CLOSE ENCOUNTERS WITH THE NEW AGE

CLOSE ENCOUNTERS
WITH
THE NEW AGE

KEVIN LOGAN

Aylesbury, Bucks HP22 5BL
ENGLAND

First published by Kingsway Publications 1991

ISBN 1 898938 28 8

British Library Cataloguing in Publication Data.
A catalogue record for this book is available from the
British Library.

Designed and Produced in England for
ALPHA an imprint of
SP Trust Ltd, Wendover Road,
Stoke Mandeville, Aylesbury, Bucks. HP22 5BL by
Nuprint Ltd, Station Road, Harpenden, Herts AL5 4SE.

Dedication

To Linda — my better half and research partner
To Peter and Cathryn — and their future

Contents

Meeting the New Age

This is a story of bright people trying to be beautiful people. It tells of a present-age people trying to break into a new age of hope and enlightenment. They are yearning for an age when humanity might evolve within and reach a higher level of consciousness and grace.

It is a new age entered by the world of inner space-travel. But many are finding that the vehicles used for these hidden, occult journeys are often rickety and ill-tested. There would be a worldwide scandal if people were sent into outer space in crafts that were equally unproved and untested.

This book could have been a cold, sober survey of a new phenomenon of our times. But such an analysis would have lost sight of the people. We would not have been able to meet Jenny, the young single parent who fights hard for her kids in a poorer part of our capital as she seeks richness and satisfaction within. There are also Tom and Renata, Terry and Marjorie, Christina and Helen and the others, all fighting to escape the cocoon of materialism in which they have been nurtured. Each in his or her own way wants to spread wings and fly from the rat race and the hypocrisy and boredom of possessions and things.

They fly inward and downward, attuning to the deep self, perhaps to the god within. Some journey to past lives in search of lessons for the present existence. Others look ahead to a thousand — even a hundred thousand — more lifetimes and eventually to…what? They are not really certain, but surely it must be better than the present age.

Many do recognise the remote and distant figure of some form of a creator or starting force, but he, she or it is so far away that they find it easier to concentrate on the creation which is closer to hand.

The New Age is about striving for a new self and a new world. It is a search for an existence that transcends the mundanity of a life that, for many, seems to have passed its sell-by date.

Before you journey with me into the New Age, please understand that this is not an encyclopedic tour of the movement. It is only an appetiser. This is not the last word about a phenomenon that is as complex and as subtle as life itself. It is just the first sentence.

Come with me, then, into this so-called New Age…so that you might know what you can do.

1. Into a New Age Conspiracy?

I was travelling into the New Age further and deeper than I had ever been before. And I was afraid.

The grandeur of Scotland's Grampians had passed almost unnoticed, and now the Cairngorms were but a receding graph line in the rear-view mirror. At that moment, with Findhorn only a few miles ahead, I would have welcomed another mountain range separating me from my New Age destination.

I had tried to keep reassuring myself that the fear was in some part irrational. In any case, it was a totally inappropriate emotion for a researcher who was striving for cool objectivity. Of course, the New Agers at Findhorn would present no threat to me, but even so, I had taken the longer scenic route, and I knew deep down that it was not just for the views. I had set off with time to spare, yet here I was, meandering through the highland foothills, three hours late and with still another thirty miles to go.

To be fair, there was a rational side to my unease. There were, in fact, four considerable reasons which made me think more than twice about spending a week in the heart of the British New Age movement. There was the worldwide conspiracy theory for one thing, and then the reaction of other Christians to my Findhorn visit for another. There had also been the threat against my family, which had come from within a more extreme form of the occult, and though the man responsible was in custody (at least, so I thought at the time), a feeling of dread occasionally visited the back of my mind. And then there was Hannah. I could not shake the conviction that, but for the New Age and the occult, she would still be alive and well.

Somehow, it seems right to start our journey into the New Age by noting the fear that can be found at the threshold. This, after all, is where many Christians are at as they peer towards the unknown of the New Age phenomenon. It seems only proper to deal with our anxieties, not only for our own sakes, but also to be fair to New Agers themselves.

First we will look at the conspiracy theory, and my aim will be to make the movement less unknown and consequently more manageable.

This part of the story has a history, so join me as I time-travel back to that crazy, anything-goes decade of the sixties. Something significant had begun to happen in Western culture as we emerged from that wild era. The permissive fling had exhausted its first energy. The long-haired flower-power generation had swapped their psychedelic Beetles for sedate saloon cars and exchanged their beads for brief-cases. The rebels had dropped back into the affluent society and, amazingly, had begun to create the most materialistic age the world had ever known. But what they did not lose was their outlook on life — a world-view glimpsed first through mind-bending LSD trips, mantra-induced meditations and magic mushrooms. It was a mindset that was beginning to saturate modern industry, commerce, education and politics as the reformed beatniks of the sixties gained respectability and promotion.

By the late seventies, culture commentators were

beginning to pick up the 'vibes'. They began buzzing
about a new consciousness; a different, higher plane of
thinking and feeling to which man might aspire. Perhaps
this was to be the next step on the ladder of evolution,
when man would truly become superman, or even realise
that he was an offshoot of the divine. Whatever the force
or spirit of the age, it was still nameless at this embryonic
stage. It caused researcher and writer Marilyn Ferguson to
speculate about 'The Movement That Has No Name',
concerning which she wrote, 'It seems to speak of
something very old. And perhaps, by integrating magic,
science, art and technology, it will succeed where all the
king's horses and all the king's men failed.'[1]

Four years later, this observation developed into a
bestseller entitled *The Aquarian Conspiracy*, in which the
author spoke of a movement with little leadership but
with a rapidly expanding international network of like-
minded people. For her, it was a benign conspiracy of
love, as people shared their inner discoveries and the
realisation that they had 'to move into the unknown: for
the known has failed us too completely'.[2]

The 'unknown' turned out to be every occult technique
known to history, plus a few fresh ones to fit the new age.
To reach the new levels of consciousness it was necessary
to connect with anything from astrology to Zen
Buddhism, plus a whole alphabet of weird and mystical
practices in between.

Those who used these techniques or systems to alter
their states of consciousness began to link together in an
atmosphere of co-operation. It was kindred spirit rather
than conspiracy which drew them together. As they did
so, and as they voyaged through inner space to find their
new and elevated selves, it seemed to them as though a
new stage in man's consciousness was about to develop.
Gradually, it came to be known as the New Age, much to

the distaste of those involved. Firstly, they hated to be labelled and secondly, they believed the label had been caricatured by the media into an umbrella term for anything that was slightly weird. However, like it or not, they and we are stuck with it.

When Christian commentators began to evaluate the movement and analyse what was involved, some could see nothing but a conspiracy.

It is 'an unparalleled mystical conspiracy threatening today's world', writes Caryl Matrisciana in *Gods of the New Age*.[3] Hal Lindsay states that 'the West has been invaded by the East' and 'every Christian must be equipped to meet the onslaught of Eastern thought'.[4]

Christian lawyer Constance Cumbey goes a step further in *The Hidden Dangers of the Rainbow* when she writes of a 'coming age of barbarism', and describes the New Age as a 'viable movement that truly meets the scriptural requirements for the Antichrist and the political movement that will bring him on the world scene'.[5]

Roy Livesey, one of the first New Age commentators in England, states that to understand the movement is to witness the 'preparations for Antichrist's One World Government'. His books contain 'an exposé of Satan's secret rulers on earth' and a strong 'plea for discernment in the Church'.[6]

Walter Martin, who began lecturing on the coming of the New Age in America thirty-five years ago and is now dead, wrote of the 'New Age holocaust' sweeping across the United States and crippling the church's witness. The New Age cult, he claimed, was 'the world of occultic darkness and spiritual danger beyond belief'.[7]

Tex Marrs in *Dark Secrets of the New Age* describes the New Age as 'Satan's plan for a one-world religion'. He claims to reveal a secret plan, part of which involves the movement waging 'a total war against Christian believers'.

The ultimate goal is to 'eliminate every vestige of Christianity'.[8]

Not only the Christian commentators caused me anxiety as I drove ever more slowly towards one of the leading world New Age centres near a tiny fishing village off the Moray Firth. The occult writers also had me worried. At the very root of the New Age was a plan to take over the planet and establish the New World Order and eliminate Christianity in the process.

In any investigation of the New Age, paganism or the occult, it is not long before the name of Madame Helena Petrovna Blavatsky surfaces. She is one of the New Age bedrocks and a much quoted source and authority today, even though she died nearly a century ago. In 1875, she founded the Theosophical Society, with the twin aims of putting Christianity and science in their places and teaching them to 'respect their Indian betters'. Several publications came from the society, including *Isis Unveiled* and *The Secret Doctrine*, both produced in trance states and automatically written under the guidance of the 'Masters'. These 'Masters' were said to be the hidden wise men who were spread around the world with the aim of bringing in a New World Order.

Rector's wife Annie Besant took over the society in 1891, aided and abetted by Alice Bailey and Rudolph Steiner. (Steiner later broke away to form a humanistic version of theosophy called anthroposophy.) Their combined literary works, strongly influenced by psychic and occultic philosophies, continued to lay a strong foundation for New Age thinking. A publishing company called Lucifer (now renamed the Lucis Trust) was established in 1922 to distribute literature to an increasing network of New Age groups. The stated goals were to establish a New World Order which would prepare the way for the New World messiah, the Lord Maitreya. They also aimed for the elimination of dogmatic religions, such as Christianity, and the establishment of a one-world government and religion. The New World Order would include a universal credit card system,[9] the use of the figures 666 (the mark of the Beast in Revelation 13:18) and an all-planet food authority and tax system.

All this information tumbled around my mind as I travelled north towards the leading light in the modern-day New Age movement. Tens of thousands of groups and organisations looked towards the Findhorn community for illumination. Each may have had different ways of expressing the New Age, as diverse as the colours of the rainbow (the symbol commandeered by the movement), but the vast majority looked to Findhorn for inspiration.

I spoke with other Christians and asked their advice as to whether or not I should go. Many frowned and spoke of courting the devil. Others said they would pray about it. They were obviously as nervous about the prospect as I was.

I decided to do what many Christians do when they don't really want to do something. I put out a really difficult fleece. If the Lord wanted me to go, then he would provide the unaffordable £180 fee for what Findhorn called their 'Experience Week' course. It made me feel comfortable and safe. Less than a month later, Doug Harris from the Reachout Trust, with his beaming, bushy face, was offering to cover all my expenses.

'You write the book and we'll pay for Findhorn,' he challenged, while standing at his trust's exhibition stall at Spring Harvest.

'Oh no,' said I. 'It wouldn't be right to take the trust's money.'

Doug managed a patient smile as my wife and I walked away. He had been praying for a suitable book to use with those who needed help on the New Age. He had already used one of my previous books, *Paganism and the Occult*,[10] with those caught up in witchcraft and satanism.

What was needed, he and I had agreed at a previous meeting, was a balanced, objective view of the British New Age scene to set alongside the dozens or so that had been imported from the United States. The American material was useful up to a point, but discerning British readers had long ago learned to take the views of their transatlantic cousins with a large pinch of salt. This was perhaps unfair on two or three of the American books, but what was certainly needed was for somebody to come alongside indigenous New Agers: to speak with them; to listen and relate to them; to draw an accurate and detailed picture of what was happening in a Britain heading for a new millennium.

'You'd be hopeless living by faith!' My wife looked at me sideways as we left Doug wondering how pigheaded some Christians could be. Linda, much my better half in matters of faith, was not going to let it rest. 'You're like that drowning man who prays for help and then sends away two rescue vessels because he's sure God's going to come down himself and save him.'

Before the end of the day, I was back at the Reachout stand saying thank you to Doug and the Lord and preparing mentally to head north, while wondering how much prayer support I could muster.

2. The Occult Link

The human mind has its flights of fancy from time to time and mine was no different as I breasted the last foothill and caught my first glimpse of the Moray Firth. A small gnat had cadged a lift through the open car window, and I suddenly saw myself as a suicidal fly dive-bombing a spider's web. I smiled at the melodramatic picture as I descended towards Findhorn, and the rational side of my mind swatted it to one side.

And yet whenever I thought of the death threat, and then of Hannah, not forgetting the alleged conspiracy, I faltered and another telegram prayer for protection was dispatched heavenward.

At this point, perhaps I should clarify my position regarding the New Age and the occult in case I might seem to be jumping to conclusions before my Scottish week had even begun. I was certainly not travelling to Findhorn to research the grey area that lies between, and links, the New Age and the occult. Long, painful counselling of victims had already established for me, beyond a shadow of a doubt, the reality of such a link. The stories of our death threat assailant and of Hannah not only explain part of my fears, but also powerfully illustrate the connection between the New Age and the occult.

To avoid any other misunderstandings, I am not

implying that New Agers are into death threats or the nastier depths of the occult world. I am simply stating that there is a connection — similar perhaps to the link between soft and hard drugs: one can lead to the other. The soft form can often seem harmless and non-threatening, but can in reality be a preparation for the hard stuff. In other words, I understand the New Age to be well towards the top of what can be an irresistibly slippery occult slope. The death threat and Hannah both originated with seemingly harmless inclinations.

The threat was one of half-a-dozen which I and my family had received in the course of an evangelistic ministry to an array of witches, satanists and New Agers. To put them in true perspective, they were not the norm. We had become friends, or at least acquaintances, of quite a few in the occult world, and some had even sent Christmas greetings (Wassal cards, actually) during the research and publication of *Paganism and the Occult*. We had listened to them long and patiently and they had eventually extended the same courtesy to us, enabling us to share our faith in Jesus. The first principle of evangelism was never more important: people need to relate to Christians before they can connect with Christ.

A few months after the publication of the book, the atmosphere began to change when we met the first of what proved to be a long trail of the tragic victims of ritual abuse; some of the children were as young as four and five. There are few things more chilling and sickening than to listen to a youngster talking of the horrors inflicted upon him by dad and an assortment of 'uncles and aunts'. The women's stories — at the time of writing nearly five dozen have come forward with appalling tales of torture, child abuse and sacrifice — were equally harrowing.

This is not the place to go into detail on this subject, and much of it has already entered the public domain through the heroic work of people like Maureen Davies, the Reachout Trust, the Evangelical Alliance coalition on the occult, and many secular agencies like the NSPCC and various branches of the social services. Suffice it to note that on the day I left for Findhorn a self-styled satanist was due to appear before the crown court to answer charges that he had threatened the life of myself and a local newspaper editor.

Mark[1] was a sad victim in two ways. First, he had become interested in New Age ideas and philosophies and then had descended to a form of do-it-yourself satanism. When we first met, his beliefs contained more of the New Age than of the hard-core occult. He was a loner, delving into his own inadequate psyche and trying to muster up some confidence in himself to cope with the outside world.

His own need for attention and the questionable ethics of a journalist made him an even more tragic victim of life. Mark rather unwisely boasted to an evening newspaper reporter about his satanism and even took the pressman into his cellar to show them his newly constructed magic circle-cum temple. Afterwards, the reporter telephoned me for my opinion on satanism. I assumed that it was a general query and spoke to him of the damage it was doing to people's personalities, and then commented about the growing evidence of ritual abuse involving children. These quotes were then inserted into the story, linking Mark with the child abuse, something I am sure Mark would never have entertained. In fact, to be fair, the vast majority within paganism and the occult are equally as horrified as Christians at child abuse.

Following weeks and months of insults and attacks from his self-righteous neighbours and the refusal of the newspaper to print a correction, Mark understandably became mentally disturbed and began a twisted campaign of threats. I had tried unsuccessfully to correct the injustice, both with the newspaper and later with the police when Mark was arrested. I was hoping it would be resolved in court, though I had been assured that Mark would be held over for further reports because of his condition.

On the morning he was due to appear before the crown court, I left for Findhorn knowing that I had done all that I could and knowing that it would be safe to leave my family for a week. Unknown to me, the court dealt with him on the day and gave him his freedom on the understanding that he kept well away from those he had threatened. He was to report back to the court in six months' time. As I write, with five of those months gone, the court's decision seems to have been right. Thankfully, the newspaper report of the court case presented a fair account of what had happened and vindicated Mark to a certain extent.

In the midst of these threats, Hannah came to stay. She was one of the half-dozen women caught up in satanism whom we have taken in en route to safe houses in different parts of the country. Her tragic story indicates the link between the occult and the New Age and the consequent problems that I might have to face if indeed there was some form of conspiracy afoot at Findhorn.

I recall one morning with particular poignancy. Hannah lay in the intensive care unit five miles away from our vicarage, her lungs deliberately paralysed so that the life-support machine could do its job.

I had returned from one of my frequent visits and was in the study talking to esoteric Mike, an ardent advocate of the New Age movement, and Pauline, who hung on each word uttered by her guru. The bleak link between the New Age and the occult came home to me more forcefully than ever before as we talked. Hannah was where she was partly because of the philosophy and activities of people like these two casual, almost hippy-like, forty-year-olds. The fruit of the Holy Spirit was wilting within and I tried to be pleasant about the New Age which had put this bonny twenty-four-year-old girl on the critical list.

'He's all around,' enthused Mike about his god-force. 'He's in us. He's in everything. He IS everything.' Pauline nodded in the obedient disciple mode.

'The one-ism of monism,' I smiled, striving for a lightness that I did not feel.

It was amazing how all these New Agers were alike when it came to basics. They all pretended to be free spirits, doing their own things, attuning to their own inner consciousnesses, yet they all sounded the same, as though they had been programmed in some subtle way. Talk to any New Ager and you will inevitably meet a monist, a pantheist or a panentheist. Monism states that everything in the universe is one; monism is one-ism. Pantheism adds a rider: all is God — you and I, the plants, our pet dog, the tree against which it wees, planet Earth, the universe, the whole shooting-match. What is, is God! Panentheism takes a sophisticated step on from there, declaring that God is *in* everything.

Some New Agers talk of God while others speak of a force of nature that has a thousand names. They include cosmic force, life-force, life-essence, etheric (that which lends substance to life), Kundalini serpent force (said to be coiled round the base of the spine), ch'i (Chinese form of universal energy), prana (the Hindu version), Brahma (the energy consciousness of our solar system), od (magnetic force), celestial hierarchies (a chain of life-giving spiritual beings), sakti (energy of the gods) and elemental essence (a formless essence reflecting the sum of all human thought). Whatever the name, New Agers tend to believe that all is one and that one is a god or force or whatever.

By contrast, orthodox Christian belief declares that God created, and then looked on his creation from outside and 'saw that it was good' (Gen 1:10,21,25,31). There is a great difference between the Creator and his creation. God might be in his creation but he is also above and apart from it (Is 57:15).

Esoteric Mike went on to the logical conclusion of his beliefs: 'We need only reach within to find the divine, to realise we ourselves are God.'

When you believe that everything is one and God is everything, it stands to reason for the New Ager that he IS God. I recalled some relevant words in Shirley MacLaine's best-selling autobiography *Out on a Limb*. Miss MacLaine, the world-famous actress and leading celebrity and promoter of New Age ideas, approvingly quotes one of her gurus as follows:

> The skeptic's view of higher knowledge of self is most limiting. Your dogmatic religions, for example, are most limiting for mankind because they demand unquestioned reverence for authority. YOU are God. YOU know you are divine. But you must continually remember your Divinity and, most important, act accordingly.[2]

Mike began to explain how new humanity needed to plumb the depths of the psyche to find the divine, using mind-expanding, mind-altering techniques such as hypnosis, drugs, meditation and various forms of divination.

I began to tell him how a girl called Hannah had reached into herself using similar techniques and ended up with a personality in shreds, totally confused, abused and lost to the point of taking a massive overdose of drugs. I hoped Mike and Pauline couldn't detect the tight anger in my throat.

Hannah had grown up in a society which had increasingly explored inner space in dangerous vehicles such as transcendental meditation, hypnotic regression, trance-channelling, astral projection, seances, astrology, yoga, tarot cards and the ouija board.

My own small research into the effects of using untried and untested occult/New Age techniques has uncovered many more deaths — at least thirty major crimes, including murder, torture, child abuse and sacrifice. Each of the crimes has recently come before British crown courts and all were committed by people who lost control because they messed about with these inner space crafts. I personally know also of some related suicides, and a few others who have effectively lost their normal lives through mental illness. I suspect that if extensive research was done into this area many more casualties might be revealed.

Through occult techniques, Hannah had come into contact with a power she could not understand, she certainly could not control, and which eventually took charge of her. During the four days that I had known Hannah before she took the overdose, she had thrown herself — and the two women counsellors with whose arms she was linked — into the path of an oncoming car on Brighton promenade. I had been walking a few yards in front and as I turned to see the cause of the commotion I saw the car swerve to avoid the sprawled figures. Some hours later, in a nearby vicarage, Hannah had slashed one of her wrists. This was the power in charge of her life, the power that many pioneer New Agers are encouraged to contact as they seek the god within and attune themselves to the cosmic life-force.

On a superficial level, these techniques seem attractive to those fleeing an ultra-materialistic society in which gold outweighs the soul. For some, it provides hope in the lostness of their worlds. Surely, as the New Age of Aquarius dawns, they reckon, a new humanity might learn to carry each other's burdens in an inner quest for peace and goodwill. We can all pursue ecological harmony and work for a New World Order. There are increasing numbers in Britain who, like Hannah, have trod the alternative paths only to come to grief on explosive mines hidden beneath the surface of this pop culture. It is important to note some of these mines.

First, the occultic means to achieve New Age ends have left many lost in confusion. Their personalities have been altered, and not for the better. Hannah was only one of the countless many who come to Christian ministers for help.

Second, the New Age is today providing a 'soft-occult' climate in which satanism and witchcraft can seem acceptable. Hannah certainly saw them as the next stage of inner growth.

Third, if the god-force is everything and everything makes up the god-force, then there is no external absolute against which to measure what is right and wrong. Truth is reduced to personal whim, and chaos and anarchy of life result. More about this in Chapter 9.

For an increasing number like Hannah, the combination of the occult with the loss of ethics and morals is proving too much. In my previous research into the areas of paganism and the occult, I had begun to notice a direct correlation between the ever-encroaching New Age and the modern boom in the occult. Those who started off in the 'soft' New Age were frequently graduating to the 'hardcore' of witchcraft and satanism. One of Hannah's jobs, before she fled satanism for Christ, had been to lure other youngsters from Euston Station, rock festivals and similar pick-up points, using New Age, soft-occult tricks, like telling futures with tarot cards or pendulum swinging. This came easily to her. It was the way she herself had first entered the occult scene.

The New Age has now become an unwitting front for the hard-core occult. The New Age is merely the old age of paganism and Eastern religions given a face-lift and a fresh application of make-up. It is a face of the decade and is already winning over the media. Television and radio, glossy magazines and the press, social commentators and style-setters are boldly plugging into the New Age fashion, without realising the dangerous occult connections. As a consequence, many more are getting caught up.

David, a twenty-year-old unemployed lad, wanted excitement and became enmeshed through acid house parties run on New Age lines. The psychiatric hospital has now allowed him to be a day-patient as he continues to recover from the severe effects of drug-taking. He took the drugs Ecstasy and LSD in order to attain the 'altered state of consciousness' necessary in the New Age to contact the 'life-force of nature'. Bill, a works manager, came seeking help after his life fell to pieces through delving into the occult, courtesy of the New Age. This paragraph could go on to fill the rest of the book.

These people began to recover after deliverance and counselling. The Holy Spirit ministered to each in a powerful way, helping them to see that there is a greater Force behind nature's force. That Force has the face of love, demonstrating that love is not impersonal.

And then there are those like Hannah. She had come to us homeless, a Christian refugee fleeing the horrors of the occult. She was depressed after a lifetime of abuse and rejection in covens and satanic temples. She was also haunted by the terrible atrocities she had committed during the rituals.

'I can't stand the screams of the children in my head,' she kept crying when things were really bad. She had become a Christian some months before and she was frequently overwhelmed by memories of what she had been involved in. She knew that Jesus had forgiven her, and often she almost felt forgiven. But the one thing she struggled with incessantly was forgiving herself. As part of self-imposed spiritual therapy, or just good old-fashioned repentance, she was preparing to go to the police even though she feared the outcome. She had even written part of her life story so that other youngsters might learn from her mistakes. The morning after arriving at our vicarage, she swallowed the contents of a drug bottle which she had kept well hidden.

The last time I saw Hannah she lay in a valley in the shadow of monitors and digital dials. They no longer flickered. The robotic click of the ventilator was no more. Hannah had come round twice during intensive care. I had talked of God's love and forgiveness. Hannah's tears seemed to end in a smile of peace…and heaven.

At the inquest some days later, the true cause of death was not recorded on the coroner's certificate. Neither the New Age nor the occult was mentioned.[3]

3. I See No Conspiracy!

M y head swivelled from side to side as I negotiated the sleeping policemen guarding the driveway up to Findhorn. Where, I wondered, were the forty-two-pound cabbages, the sixty-pound broccoli and the eight-foot delphiniums grown under the guidance of the devas' spirits?

There had been many stories of 'people who talk to plants with amazing results — stories of vegetable and flower gardens animated by angelic forms where Pan's pipes are heard in the wind — stories of plants performing incredible feats of growth and endurance'.[1] There was also a man called Roc, who could sit for hours chatting with Pan and other nature spirits, and embracing the plants with love and acceptance; a man who stood face to face against the elf king.[2]

Then there were Peter and Eileen Caddy, the founders of Findhorn, and Dorothy Maclean. Dorothy was told at the beginning, 'You are to co-operate in the garden by thinking about the Nature Spirits...these beings are of the Light, willing to help but suspicious of human beings.'[3]

Eileen, apparently the only one of the original trio remaining at the time of my visit, put it all at God's door, but from what I had heard, the God she referred to was different from the God described in the Bible.

As I parked the car — taking much longer than was necessary — yet another thought niggled its way to the front of my mind. One of the foundation pillars of the New Age was the ancient occultic practice of astrology. In fact, the public were first introduced to the New Age through this medium via the smash-hit musical *Hair!* Its lyrics and tunes celebrated the dawning of the 'Age of Aquarius' and had a whole nation chanting 'Hare Krishna' for months.

It was the first taste of an age in which, *Hair!* prophesied, governments and countries would fall or be changed, society and family would expire and a new order would rise up out of the ashes of old values and beliefs. Looking at the disintegration of modern family life, the ever-changing scene of world politics and the death of right and wrong ethics, the age which *Hair!* foretold is not far away!

Underlying the musical, and indeed the whole New Age movement, are the astrological ages of man; each age is said to last about two thousand years. One popular explanation of the ages goes like this: Adam was the herald of the Taurean Age (the age of the bull which gives life), while Abraham began the age of Aries (sacrificing the ram instead of his son). Jesus Christ brought in the Piscean Age (hence the *ichthus* fish sign of the early church and the numerous allusions to fishermen being turned into fishers of men).

As we approach the close of this present two-thousand-year span, we are told to look forward to the Age of Aquarius, the water-carrier. This is the age of service, sharing, loving, and caring and the age when man must be prepared to help himself. There is also the thought that we are inheritors of all that has gone before and that we become all that those ages represented. The first age was said to belong to God the Father, the second to God the Son and the last age to God the Spirit. Now is the dawning of fulfilled man, who takes in all the Trinity and becomes one with the Divine. All we need to do now, we are told, is to wake up to the fact that we are God.

The true Aquarian is said to be friendly, progressive, creative, inventive, independent, original, tolerant, refined, artistic, discreet, optimistic and fond of science and literature. The New Ager certainly seems to have used all these qualities in creating and refining an original artistic fiction. It often seems that the New Ager has invented his 'science' independently of any authority except that of optimistic inner influences and lumps of matter whizzing through space.

What had I driven into?

Fear distorts perspective, rather like assessing yourself and your situation in one of those wobbly fairground mirrors. We Christians tend to have a whole hall of crazy mirrors as we picture ourselves in the world. We peer out from our cosy fellowships at the continually changing, often alarming, world and our little fears become magnified into an illusion of horrors, causing us to shrink from our Christ-given commission. We are to go to every corner of the world, including Findhorn. God so loved the New Agers there that he gave his only Son for them. He loved them so much that he commanded his followers to go.

Part of my journey to Findhorn was evangelistic. My personal, self-imposed brief was to test out some ways of communicating the good news of Jesus Christ among a people who accepted the New Age concept of the cosmic Christ as gospel. But I was also there to find out, to understand, to discover, to learn and to research. As a trained journalist (before entering the Christian ministry), I had an innate distrust of second-hand information which could often become tainted in the retelling. What I most wanted was a true picture of the New Age in action, not others' second-hand caricatures. British Christianity needed most of all a view of the British New Age scene rather than an American paperback view, which, though useful, was often much more than an ocean away from its British expression.

Findhorn was the next stage in a journey of personal investigation which had already taken my wife and me to Glastonbury, the occult and New Age centre of Britain. We had experienced Earthweek, when hundreds of New Agers, witches and pagans had gathered, some in their tepees, near the tor, to raise awareness that the planet was 'one living whole'.[4] Quite a few had been on the now famous Harmonic Convergence, when hundreds of thousands had gathered at sacred sites around the world to stage a 'hum-day', harmonising the universal vibrations to save the world.[5] There had also been the London Festival of Mind, Body and Spirit, which is to New Agers what Keswick and Spring Harvest are to many Christians.

Also on the schedule, already dealt with or pending, were St James, Piccadilly (the New Age in Church of England dress); Monkton Wylde and the Wrekin Trust (both similar in some ways to Findhorn); the Glastonbury Festival of Contemporary Performing Arts; and Tara Centre, with Benjamin Creme playing the part of a modern-day John the Baptist preparing the way for the return of the messiah — the Lord Maitreya. There were also many other smaller events, people and writings which made up my research.

The sprawl of caravans, huts, mock-Swiss chalets and whisky-barrel-shaped homes that is Findhorn at last filled the windscreen panorama. Like it or not, I was here. I could still turn round on what appeared to be an old runway, stretching away to the neighbouring property of

Kinloss RAF base. As I pondered the choice, the nearby roar of a radar reconnaissance Nimrod with its protruding bulbous nose gave me a comforting feeling that the normal world was not too far away. In any case, the visit was not the idiotic risk it might seem to some. There was, I reassured myself, no inextricable conspiracy awaiting.

Perhaps I should explain why the rational side of my brain insisted on overriding some of the fears we have so far looked at. I did, and still do, have substantial difficulties accepting the existence of a worldwide New Age conspiracy, at least at the human level.

I have majored on this conspiracy and its associated fears because I believe it can destroy future evangelism in the New Age. It is vital for Christians to see this thriving new subculture in a balanced perspective. Nothing is more guaranteed to sink the British New Ager beneath waves of laughter than the oft-repeated Christian claim of a worldwide plot. Nothing, I believe, damages our credibility and integrity more. Let us see what some of the more balanced Christian commentators on the New Age think.

Michael Cole writes in *What Is The New Age?*:

> I have sought to be open to the possibility that there is a world conspiracy. I have quoted from original sources, and I have tried to build a strong case. At times I have almost persuaded myself that what these people wrote is true — that the ultimate goal of the New Age is world domination.

Cole does see the New Age as 'a very significant shift in mankind's world-view', but he concludes that there is no organisational human conspiracy, even while suspecting it to be an 'unholy alliance' challenging the authority of God.[6]

Elliot Miller, in his scholarly *A Crash Course on the New*

Age Movement, for which I was privileged to contribute the British foreword, makes a substantial critique of the conspiracy theory, concluding:

> It is time for the Church to wake up fully, shaking off its dreamy fantasy of a monolithic New Age conspiracy. Only then can it truly rise up to the very real and formidable challenges of the New Age movement.[7]

Eric Pement, in his New Age assessment *Consensus or Conspiracy*, comments:

> Conspiracy theories are a dime a dozen, and none of them should cause us to put down the sickle and take up the spyglass. If we must have a conspiracy, then let us be part of it — an invading fifth column, working toward the final overthrow of darkness. Our words and actions should therefore spring not from paranoia of the times, but from the forthright love and boldness of God.[8]

Douglas R. Groothius, in *Unmasking the New Age*, states:

> …the New Age movement is better viewed as a world-view than a global conspiracy. This is not to minimise its influence but to recognise it as an intellectual, spiritual and cultural force to be reckoned with in all sobriety.[9]

As I had prepared to journey to Findhorn with much knowledge gained already of New Agers, the rational side of my mind was almost confident that there was no conspiracy afoot. Having met and talked with many of the New Age leaders and gained experience of various groups and activities, such a conspiracy would have gone against all that I judged that the New Age stood for.

At the heart of the New Age is one simple rule: everybody does what is right in his or her own eyes. The New Age revolves around the individual and the transformation of self. Certainly, it has a global awareness, and there is a great call to transform society. But the whole movement is, remarkably, without leadership and when the more charismatic types get too pushy, others are quick to remind them that they have no authority whatsoever. In fact, an authority external to one's own individual authority does not exist.

All New Agers consider themselves to be parts of the cosmic, universal consciousness or force. They are the Ultimate Authority, if there is such a thing. Consequently, no one part has any right to tell another part what to do. Commandments, orders, laws, rules, domination and authority are words with little meaning on a personal level in the New Age. They fall before the vocabulary of harmony, co-operation, sharing, togetherness, agreement, accord and consensus. It is all done by attuning to each other's wavelengths and becoming one on a given subject. The concept of an autocratic or dictatorial leadership is laughable.

When it comes down to comparing the various foundations and groups, there is an underlying likeness in philosophies, and certainly there is co-operation and even a benign conspiracy. But the practical expressions of the ideas are often as different as chalk is from cheese.

For the Christian, this represents the biggest headache, and at the same time provides a base for the greatest criticism of the New Age. The headache comes from the impossibility of encapsulating the New Age in a few sentences. The New Age chameleon changes depending on its background. The movement consequently defies labelling because by the time you have finished explaining the label you have written a book.

At the same time, this presents Christians with a vital challenge to the New Age. With so many differences, distinctions and even contradictions within the New Age, who is to know who, or what, is right? If what is right is down to personal whim or greed or pride, isn't that an outrageous recipe for anarchy, and the disintegration of society?

There is no organised structure and even the networks, involving tens of thousands of groups, are a loosely organised chaos. The whole idea of a New Age is that autocratic and authoritative organisations, governments and structures of the past have not worked. The known way of the old age is redundant. Now it is time to move into the unknown.

A human-based conspiracy? No.

But that, of course, is not the last word for Christians. We contend not only with flesh and blood, for there is also in the spiritual realms a conspiracy of evil older than the ages themselves. It is aerial warfare in the heavenlies 'against the rules, against the authorities, against the powers of this dark world and against the spiritual forces of evil' (Eph 6:12). Certainly, Christians are assured that they are on the winning side and that Christ has destroyed the devil's works (1 Jn 3:8); that Christ, rather than the devil, has all the authority (Col 1:15 – 20) and that God is in overall charge (Ps 24:1). But the Christian still stands vulnerable in the midst of the battle zone needing full armour-plated cover (Eph 6:11; 2 Cor 2:11).

Whatever I faced at Findhorn, I was mighty glad that dozens of prayer warriors were battling back at home and in many parts of the country on my behalf, even as I sat in my parked car on the runway.

The ensuing chapters will take you through the diary of events that followed.

4. People of the New Age

Saturday evening

Sixteen pairs of eyes encircle me. Their owners want to know my spiritual story; where am I coming from? What am I into? What do I want from Findhorn?

I quietly thank God that I had resisted the fleeting temptation to come as an undercover Christian spy. This week is obviously to be a soul-baring exercise: no room for sham. It is to be group dynamics at its most soul-searching — the very nub of the New Age business, as I am to discover. The word has apparently already got round that they have a writer-vicar in their midst. Now the eyes wait expectantly.

One strikingly blue pair, set in a boyish, tanned face with surrounding hair and wispy beard grown in the 'Hollywood Jesus' style, belongs to Mike. He's in his mid-twenties and heavily into reincarnation with Buddhist leanings. He has taken the week off from a 7,000-mile, two-year trek round the British coastline ('Only the east coast left to do!'). He has only a few pounds left to his name, and Findhorn has given him an assisted place from its bursary fund while the rest of us are paying between £180 – £230 'as we felt led'.

The group wait for me after listening to Mike's story. I

36

had warmed to him, for not only was he a fellow Lancastrian but he was deliberately transparent and sincere in his searching. As he picked his way along the thin Middle Way of Buddhism, the self-imposed resolve and concentration of the tight-rope walker was evident in his careful, slow speech. Here, incarnated in the flesh before me, was a fair attempt at the eightfold path of Right Speech, Right Action, Right Views, Right Intent, Right Livelihood, Right Effort, Right Mindfulness and Right Concentration. It was the narrow, tricky path of the Buddha, based on the Four Truths: that life is suffering, desire causes suffering, suffering dies with desire and the Noble Eightfold Path is the only way to bury desire.

A hard life — or rather, lives, for enlightenment is inextricably linked to the never-ending, ever-turning wheel of reincarnation. Each disciple works out his *karma*, enjoying or enduring the consequences of every thought and deed of lives past, present and to come. In spite of this, there was a sparkle of hope in Mike's eyes as he told his story. For him, what he now had was preferable to the emptiness of his lost materialistic teens in down-town Blackburn.

Suddenly, I cared greatly for this man, who seemed to embody the essence of the seeking, searching, spiritually hungry New Age. As I listened, I mused in my sadness that I had found Jesus Christ and eternal life at a church five miles from Mike's home, in the neighbouring town of Accrington. He, on the other hand, had travelled 5,000 miles to India for a revelation that promised an eternity of striving for no known purpose.

His are one pair of eyes which now wait on me. How am I to share a testimony involving a loving Saviour and resurrection to eternal life, a total denial and contradiction of Mike's story?

In fact, as I had listened to the others in the group, my

spiritual pilgrimage had contradicted just about everybody else's story. All had spoken of a journey in one form or another. All saw life as an ongoing search — another essential nub, it seemed, of the New Age movement. There was no sure destination, only a voyage into some unknown future.

Now that it was my turn to speak, I was going to tell of a desperate search that ended in the abundant life provided by Christ. Certainly, I was still a pilgrim and there was, thank the Lord, infinitely more to discover and treasure, but at least I knew where I was going. In such a group as this, wouldn't such a declaration sound incredibly superior and intolerant, even though I would simply be repeating the promises Jesus had given to his followers?

I had felt an overwhelming oneness with the stories of two in the circle, although again my story was going to be a rejection of theirs. Terry, in his late forties like myself, is the co-focaliser of the group and as such is the one through whom, and in whom, the energy of the group is focused. A focaliser is not a leader, it must be stressed. ('We are all leaders of ourselves…'. So much for theories about a conspiracy with strong directive leadership.)

Terry and I, it turned out, were both lapsed Roman Catholics, the same as Christina, single and thirtyish, from London. The three of us had actually found each other during the previous informal get-to-know-each-other cup of tea. We had settled in and swapped background tales, all three being victims of the pre-Vatican II, Irish and superstitious type of Catholicism.[1] We had chuckled in close identity with each other as I had shared my 'foolproof' way of getting to heaven…

'As a normal teenager with an overactive, virile imagination, I figured I was in mortal sin every time a member of the opposite sex walked past me.' The others had smiled and nodded in full harmony with similar memories. (For the record, mortal sins — anything terribly bad, like impure thoughts and murder — blackened the soul and, if unconfessed, meant a direct descent to hell on death. Present-day forms of Catholicism, especially the charismatics, lay much more stress on the loving, forgiving and accepting nature of God.)

'Anyway,' I continued, 'the only way I believed I would ever get to heaven was by going to confession as late as possible on a Saturday evening, performing a perfect penance of prayers, rushing home to bed and taking a sleeping-pill so that I'd have no naughty dreams. I would then arise for the early workers' Mass, take the Communion host and say a short prayer afterwards. With all this done perfectly, I would gain the plenary indulgence that wiped away the punishment for all my sins.' By this time, the other two were nodding vigorously, remembering their own inability to keep the laws and avoid hell.

'I then reckoned,' I concluded, 'that having done all that was necessary to get myself into a state of grace, I needed just one small stroke of luck outside church — to get knocked down by a double-decker bus!'

Smiles. No guffaws of laughter for us, lapsed Catholics all three. The memories were too painful and had robbed us of too many precious years.

Terry had told us that his search for an alternative god or philosophy after leaving the church went on for two decades before it eventually brought him to his present stage as a member of the staff of Findhorn.

As for Christina, she was still looking, a refugee from a churchianity which had taught her about spirituality and God while at the same time placing them both well beyond reach. Having dumped a God who dangled her over the pit of hell, she had now come to Findhorn seeking the god within.

Sandwiched between Mike and Terry in the group that awaited my testimony is Jenny. Her story has already been retailed before the group. When I first saw her, she was like a coiled spring in jumper and slacks, waiting, it seemed, for an alarm to go off. I wouldn't have wanted to pick an argument with Jenny. Instinct hinted that there was an anger and tension simmering beneath the small, trim figure and that stern, unmadeup face. A single mum from London, Jenny had taken a break from her two kids and had returned after an interval of a year to Findhorn 'to give it another try'.

Towards the end of a story which ranged from East End communism through ardent feminism to disenchantment and questioning, Jenny smiled and suddenly a vulnerable, attractive personality blossomed from nowhere. I didn't know it then, but Jenny was to be the one with whom I would most identify during my Findhorn Experience Week. First appearances were deceptive and I was to find a warmth and compassion and humour that made her a good friend. She too was questioning.

The year before, she had been 'bowled over' by the love and openness that she had experienced during her first stay at Findhorn. There was in the community an absence of the anger which she encountered so frequently in the rush and rage of her home neighbourhood in London. She had returned to try and make sense of it all. Was it all an act? Was it for real? What did people do with the anger of life at Findhorn? Would the experience of the first visit stand up to further investigation? In many ways, Jenny would be asking similar questions to my own. We were, however, coming from different understandings and despite our friendship, it was unlikely that we would reach the same conclusions.

The eyes still look in my direction. In the circle, only six of us are English, the last one being Marjorie, a charming, open woman in her late forties and the group's other co-focaliser. The rest, mostly under forty, are a mini League of Nations.

Tom, footloose and fancy-free, from Wellington, New Zealand, had met Brigitte 'from the US of A' in Inverness two days prior to the Experience Week starting. Brigitte, a meditation specialist wanting to retune her spirit, had painted Findhorn in such attractive colours that Tom had drawled, 'What the heck, I've nothing much else to do for the next week.'

On the other hand, orchestral musicians Graham and Susan, together with Henriette, an astonishingly fit and alert seventy-year-old, felt Findhorn was worth a 1,000-mile drive from the other side of Holland. Henriette had bubbled with natural health as she told her story. She had spoken excitedly of her lakeside patch of 'pure earth' in Den Haag, an organic outpost and valiant last stand against the suicidal European onslaught of modern chemicals and pesticides. This was her little 'kingdom of God', her Garden of Eden 'complete with apple tree'.

'After many fruitful years the apple tree grew sick,' she told us sadly. 'I gave it all sorts of good biological fertilisers, but finally it became so ill I just could not look at it, you really would have cried.' Henriette's lined face mirrored her emotions as she explained how she told the tree that she would have to cut it down.

'I said to my apple tree. "What have I done wrong? I have tried to commune with you." And then I got the answer: "You always have talked with me but you never blessed me." I never understood that when divine life in a tree is given to me to care for, I have to give it back to God.'

Henriette added, 'I am a good Protestant. Call it pantheism [God is everything] if you want, but there is nothing without God. I came to Findhorn to learn how to work more practically in the garden, to see how they are doing it.'

Renata, an attractive travel agent in her mid-thirties, had been the first of the German-Austrian-Swiss contingent to speak, using a best German *Hochdeutsch* lilt. A talk by Findhorn founder Eileen Caddy in Frankfurt had first introduced her to New Age ideas a decade before, and she had now come to advance her own personal development. She totally accepted Eileen as 'one of many messengers from God' who brought 'pure love', because intuition told her it was right. She also shared that she was 'very taken with a Zen master, Baker Roshi' who taught Zen Buddhism 'which has the same God or love-message that the Christian belief has'. (This type of mixed-up theology and thinking is rampant in the New Age. Actually, Buddhism has no place for a god in its official teachings.)

The remainder of the mid-European contingent includes quiet German Gertie from Schutlerwald, schoolgirl Anette from Wolfenbuttel, with her painful broken English, and Annelies, a newly liberated but shy divorcee, from Switzerland.

From down under, there is try-anything-once Richard, a dashing, handsome twenty-year-old who seems to have time on his hands during his leisurely stroll around the world.

'Findhorn seemed an interesting place to come,' he had told us in his testimony. He was open, he said, to any new experiences and he seemed to be gathering them as if he were a collector of rare species. Come to think of it, there was a hint of this in most testimonies. Definitely a New Age trait.

Fellow Australian Helen could not have been more different in outlook. Channelled spirits were her special interest, especially Bartholomew and Emmanuel. She was also into Lazaris, the spirit famous with celebrities, and the one whom television's Sharon Gless (of *Cagney and Lacey* and *The Trials of Rosy O'Neil*) thanked for helping her to win her Emmy award for best actress.

Helen likewise was grateful, though not specifically to any one spirit, guide or guru. She preferred to keep her independence, like all the rest of the group. Helen's insistence on self was again a total contradiction to the Christian story which, of course, includes cheerfully losing self and independence to a Lord and Saviour. We Christians might not do it very well, but at least that is our ideal. Again, my testimony was going to be a contradiction.

The sixteen pairs of eyes and ears still point in my direction; still wait for details of my search.

I begin to speak of growing up with a God who didn't like me very much; who made it as difficult as possible for me to reach him. I had to negotiate with a plethora of underlings, such as priests and saints, and even then this God was lost behind a haze of incense. My human mum and dad loved me with an elastic patience that never snapped and that would never have disowned me. My heavenly Father apparently didn't go in for such sentimentality and was quite prepared to toss me into an eternal inferno if I didn't behave myself. This Father's heaven sounded too much like hell. I go on to speak of the years on the run; guilty, unhappy, empty years; a time of dissipation and lostness when the only gods worth bothering about were journalism, women and gambling.

Everybody in the group has stayed with me so far. Each

pair of eyes seems attentive and accepting and sympathetic. Not for much longer, I muse; not when I begin to speak of Jesus being 'the way, the truth and the life', and the only way to God (Jn 14:6).

As I build up to this point, I speak of the lowest pit of my life — of a spiritual vacuum, a marriage on the rocks and a wife who I at first thought had gone round the religious bend and joined those Jesus freaks. I spoke of a desperation so bad that, rather than end up with nothing, I was prepared to return to the ogre-god of my childhood and even try and convert my wife to that way in the process. Linda, however, with Jesus in her life, was not for turning.

And now for the crunch issue. I tell them of a blinding flash of inspiration which was almost audible: a realisation that hit me with astonishing force. God loved me more than any human father; more even than I loved my own recently born son. Were human fathers not, after all, made in God's image? Were we not but pale imitations of the Almighty Lord and Lover of the universe? This God wanted as much, if not more, for me than I wanted for my son. He wanted me to turn to him, to be his heir, to work for him on earth, to be with him for eternity in heaven. The blaze of enlightenment came after months of searching Scripture, long nights of religious discussion and hard days of soul-searching and wondering. Suddenly, it was as if the Spirit of God had placed all into a giant separator and squeezed out the essence of truth into my spirit.[2]

It is over, and I sit back to await the group's reaction.

'Great!' smiles focaliser Terry. 'Super!' And everybody is smiling.

'It's okay,' smile the eyes. 'Great for you, Kev, but we're into something else.'

Don't they understand? Have they not heard a word

I've said? Can they not see that life's search ends at the face of love? Salvation is there before their very eyes.

'Mike!' I want to shout. 'There is no need for a thousand and one lives to clean you up. Christ has already done it with the blood of Calvary. Life does have a purpose in God's overall plan. All you need is to surrender to him.'

The truth suddenly strikes home with a fresh force. Surrender of self is not on the menu of life in our group on this Saturday evening; only realisation of self. Self is god. Fulfilment and enlightenment of self are the goals in an existence in which knowledge is bliss and ignorance is the opposite.

The gods of the New Age are identical to those in the first age in the Garden of Eden when people told God to go to hell and refused to be told what they could and couldn't eat. Adam and Eve, the gods of the garden, reigned briefly after the serpent tempted them to eat and 'be like God'. But then had come God's coup and the man-gods were cast into the wilderness to begin their search back to God.

Members of the group, as with humanity in general, are still searching…yet never finding. They are the lost little gods of an age as old as Adam.

5. Planet of Doom, Sunday Worship and What the Dwarf Bean Spirit Said to the Gardener!

Sunday breakfast

'By the time you've finished your muesli,' accuses the voice over my shoulder, 'two hundred more babies will have been born!' I wonder if there is something I should know about the Findhorn muesli.

The owner of the voice, a Findhorn resident with whom I had swapped tales of planetary doom and gloom the previous evening, laughs and drifts on past the breakfast-table, enjoying his belated last word.

Doom-laden data pours out of New Agers faster than the birth-rate! If Christians knew their Bibles as well as these people knew their end-of-the-world scenarios, I muse, there would never have been the need for a New Age.

In the last twelve hours (eight of which I slept through) I have learned that:

- Kitchen food blenders can damage hearing at 110 decibels. West Africans at the age of seventy have better hearing than Londoners at twenty.
- Britain is one of the most densely populated countries, with 604 people per square mile. If we all went to the seaside at the same time, we'd each have four inches of sand.

- We spend nine tenths of our lives indoors cut off from nature and affected, so some experts claim, by electromagnetic circuits in our homes and offices which cause allergies, nervous disorders and high blood pressure.
- Six out of ten people are more than nine weeks behind in their mortgage repayments.
- The world will die in the year 2050 if we go on polluting and poisoning it at the present rate, according to a Massachusetts university computer.
- Most New Agers either belong to the Green Party or will vote for it at the next election (personal observation).

The family of Findhorn exists because people are fleeing a noisy, polluted, poisoned, materialistic, unspiritual, greedy, corrupt world hell-bent on the planetary equivalent of suicide.

Sunday worship?

'Don't forget our little ritual,' Terry says, smiling around the circle of 'worshippers'. Sacred dance is about to commence. We obediently make praying hands, pointing the turreted fingers away from us.

'Remember, turn your hands sideways so that the thumbs point to your right, and join hands,' encourages our focaliser. 'We take the group energy in through our fingers and pass it on through our thumbs, okay?'

Attunement, it is called; the ritual that begins and finishes every event and task we are to perform together. We are required to 'plug in' to each other and the universal energy. Every two-minute attunement found me praying for the owners of the hands I held. Rarely in the history of spiritual conflict have so many been prayed for, for so long and so often by so few (just me).

The ritual focused a truth I had previously only glimpsed: Christians in groups, hands held or not, will attune to the one personal God. New Agers, on the other hand, tune in to each other and to that life-energy with a thousand names.

'Dip, dip, sideways, dip, dip,' murmurs a dreamy Jashanna, while her lithe, six-foot dancer's frame flows gracefully and obediently to the words.

Now it is our turn. We all dip, except for one who goes sideways, and we fall like drunken dominoes! Eventually, we are dipping and gliding like veteran Greek fishermen on the Isle of Kos, for this is their welcoming dance; a slow, circular, mesmeric rhythm that is almost like chanting in motion.

'Feel the flow...let your muscles erupt into a mass of rhythm...dip, dip, sideways, dip, dip...share the life experience of the fishermen.' Jashanna's voice drifts on, drawing the dancers ever deeper into their own, and the group's, consciousness. I opt again for a chat with God, explaining to him what a great catch Jashanna would be for the local charismatic dance troupe. I know he knows, but it's something to keep my mind engaged and safe.

We leave Kos and begin a couple of 'sermons' in dance-form, with ourselves as the 'preachers'. The snake dance has three strings of people interweaving and getting all knotted-up in the process. The music stops, and we reverse out of the chaos. Positive thinking moral: what you get into, you can get out of. Next is the three-steps-forward-one-step-back dance. Positive thinking moral: in this dance of life, focus on the forward steps, not the backward one. Next is a dance of pure praise to the four elements — earth, fire, water and air. Oh dear. My ankle suddenly starts playing up.

Sunday afternoon

The grand tour; shall we at last see the gigantic broccoli? Are such things possible on a twenty-two-acre sandy spit in the Moray Firth, nearer to the Arctic Circle than it is to the south coast of England? Our South African guide, Kath, takes us on safari.

We are treated to the magical history of Findhorn, starting in the sixties when ex-squadron-leader Peter Caddy and his wife Eileen settled in a mobile home outside the village of Findhorn, later joined by Dorothy Maclean. With many mystical experiences during Eastern explorations, Peter believed God wanted him to live by faith. Messages came through the nature spirits called *devas* (a Hindu word for 'beings of light') with Dorothy as the receiver, or through Peter and Eileen's intuition. Other unnamed 'overlighting angels' were also in contact with the trio.

Hundreds of messages began to come one summer:

DWARF BEAN DEVA: The first lot [of beans] was sown too deeply and before the forces of the garden were great enough.

TOMATO DEVA: It is shivery for them, but we shall try to protect them. You can give them liquid manure now.

SPINACH DEVA: If you want strong, natural growth of the leaf, the plants will have to be wider apart than they are at the moment.

LANDSCAPE ANGEL: Do not have the idea that a sodden day like today is not good. We can use it for sending down certain forces in the raindrops.

MARROW DEVA: We are glad of the direct contact [with Dorothy]! We feel and see the forces in the garden, but the contact is also a delight — it is a novelty.[1]

'But where are the beach-ball-size cabbages?' one of the group asks.

The answer is disappointing for some. It appears that the spirits simply wanted to teach the original trio a lesson in nature co-operation.

'We don't grow the big stuff any more,' says Kath, blithely. 'That was just to show us what could be done. People began to get hung up on size and missed the real point of co-operating with the nature spirits. We have now been guided into growing people in a big way!'

Were there ever towering delphiniums, or was it all just a tall story? Many at Findhorn believed without question, though I never was able to locate a first-hand eye-witness in my week's stay. To be fair, it was twenty-odd years since the reign of the giant vegetables. All that remains today is a display of amateur black-and-white photographs which are inconclusive.

The group has to settle for an account of the bare facts about the present-day community. We learn that there are 4,000 visitors a year, with 450 members living on site or in the village. The community is run by eight elected focalisers, plus trustees and a finance group. There are twenty-eight departments, all of which begin work with a daily attunement; workers are co-creators with the spirits and work is love in action where the human consciousness can flower. Findhorn is part of a network of light, working for positive planetary change in co-operation with spiritual forces. This is part of a divine plan, access to which is gained through meditation, inner listening and visualisation, through which peace and healing are relayed back to the planet. Each community members gets an allowance of £125 a month (if they wish) and many supplement this with income from crystal healing, aromatherapy and divination by tarot and palms, or other work. The community shop is a veritable what's what in the world of occult and New Age books and artefacts. The average stay of community members is four years. There are many training courses, teaching personal interaction, self-awareness, personal growth skills and 'how to' lessons on anything from the mystical to the practical. Findhorn took off in the seventies with the arrival of David Spangler, who became chief focaliser.

One especially interesting fact emerges from the tour: Findhorn is where it is because it is believed to be a power-point in the British Isles. It is on a ley line, and many other New Age centres like Glastonbury in Somerset and Monkton Wylde in Dorset also claim this distinction.

Ley lines are said to be invisible currents running through the earth in straight lines and criss-crossing the land. They are a fairly modern idea, with their origins being in the mind of a Hereford magistrate, Alfred Wakins, in the twenties. He was a retired gentleman who suddenly began to see that significant tors and mounds and churches could be aligned with each other. Maybe, he reasoned, they were like that because they marked an old grass track, and so he called them leys, a corruption of 'leigh', which he believed meant 'grassy path'. He published his idea in 1925 — by that time enlarged to take in the whole country — in *The Old Straight Track*, and was promptly dismissed as a crank by the establishment. Popular opinion, however, turned him into a folk-hero and he even had his own fan club, called The Straight Track Postal Club. People from all over wrote in to confirm their sightings of ley lines, complete with ancient monuments and sites.

Within a decade, others noted that ley lines often went

in parallels; but why would travellers want two tracks going in the same direction for miles on end? Maps then showed that the reported ley lines formed geometric figures. Whatever they were, reasoned the 'experts', they were not likely to be roads and grassy tracks. There was also a controversy running at the same time as to what constituted a ley line. Surely anybody could simply take a line from any point and note some interesting features along the way! The 'experts' eventually decided that a ley line could only be a ley line if it linked five significant sites.

A little later, it was suggested that maybe our ley lines were similar to the Chinese 'dragon paths' (*lung mei*) which were said to carry the energy of the emperor. British dowsers were also thinking along the same lines (sorry!) and began to detect streams of energy in the earth to coincide with the ley lines.

It is amazing what humanity can dream up when the starting point is a universal cosmic energy rather than God. Eastern practices have long thought of the gods in terms of energy. The followers also concluded that as energy has to flow, so man should be able to detect, control and manipulate that flow. It was Eastern thought that gave us the 'ley lines' of the body, the invisible flows of energy which are said to be controlled by acupuncture or acupressure, or a dozen other techniques. I shall say more of this in the Appendix on New Age medicine. It was almost inevitable that a dawning New Age should invent energy flows through the earth, especially when they view the whole planet as one massive living organism of energy; I shall examine this further in Chapter 6.

Consider the following questions. Would you be bothered to hear that your church, house, workplace or whatever is built on a ley line? Have you ever wondered what the Christian response should be?

Having researched and written on paganism and the occult, I do understand that there are dangerous occult powers that we need to avoid. But might I dare suggest that the appropriate Christian response to ley lines is summed up in one word: codswallop!

We have enough to bother about in this world without worrying over the imaginary, invisible, invented meanderings of an elderly Hereford magistrate who happened to line up his local church, tor and pub in a straight line.

Sunday evening

Work!

Paying guests at around £200 each we may be, but there are the toilets and bathrooms to clean, kitchens and dining-room to service, and gardens and the *devas* to tend.

Attunement!

That is how we are to discover which vacancy to go for. We join hands, and I ask God to keep me away from the *devas* at the bottom of the Findhorn garden ('and I'm not too keen on scrubbing toilets either, Lord'). Choices 'impressed upon us' in meditation are then made.

Monday morning

I enjoy a breakfast of figs and muesli, then gladly report to the kitchen focaliser. Perhaps I can influence the menu and win double egg, sausage, bacon and beans for tomorrow's breakfast — a slim hope in a vegetarian establishment. Meat consumption brings discord, shattering harmony with nature, some New Agers believe. Others think that it blocks off inner-conscious links with the cosmic force, or it is cruelty to animals, or one of a dozen other explanations, depending on whom you talk to.

Our kitchen focaliser-chef is fresh back after two weeks' holiday with Mum and confesses her difficulty in returning to her kitchen chores. The 'angel of the kitchen' is invoked for help during attunement.

A thought strikes as I am asked if it feels right for me to clean and grate the carrots: if Christians began to accept the spiritual realm as readily as do New Agers; if they centred themselves more on Jesus Christ with the same eagerness with which New Agers plugged themselves into the force, we might just have an almighty revival on our hands one day!

'How do I get the carrots like that?' I ask, looking at the finely grated left-overs from the previous night.

'Hector,' came the reply. 'He's just behind you and his bits and pieces are on the bottom shelf.'

'Hello,' I said to a five-foot piece of machinery. 'My name's Kevin.' The focaliser shakes her head and smiles tolerantly at yet another of these hopeless Experience Week greenhorns.

As I look round, everything has a name except the kitchen sinks. For some reason they remain anonymous. In the coming week, I am to get to know each piece of equipment intimately except for Flora, Dora and Cora. They are not about to trust me near the three giant kitchen ovens.

Gaia gone mad in the kitchen, I figure.

Oh. We haven't officially been introduced to Gaia yet, have we? Allow me to present the goddess of the earth...

6. Gaia and a Fairy Story

Whenever I think of Gaia, I feel a fairy story coming on. This is not meant as a cheap jibe at the expense of New Agers. Even they themselves, in clearer moments, feel that the idea of Gaia might be pushing reality just a little too far.

Not so for Dr James Lovelock of Devon, a former NASA scientist. He was inspired by the first space pictures of our planet and came up with a new way of explaining life on earth. Not only were the plants and creatures alive and well on planet Earth, he maintained, so too was the earth 'herself'!

In two books about Gaia,1 Dr Lovelock set out to show that the earth's 'rocks, oceans and atmosphere, and all living things are part of one great organism, evolving over a vast span of geological time'.2 Dr Lovelock, who describes himself as a 'positive agnostic...too deeply committed to science for undiluted faith', obviously wanted, like many in modern science, to find a unified view of life apart from God.3

Gaia was the solution. Gaia, the Greek goddess of earth, was the name adopted by Dr Lovelock for his gigantic living entity of the earth. In his first book, he stated that the earth was a self-regulating, self-sustaining organism, one that could keep itself clean and tidy and even young looking through self-regulation.

Television biologist David Bellamy wrote of the doctor's second book: 'Open the cover and bathe in great draughts of air that excitingly argue the case that the earth is alive.'4 Not only was it alive, warned the good doctor, but if its occupants were not more attentive and careful, the earth would rise up against them and shrug them off. 'Gaia is not always the benign life-force many people have taken her to be,' he adds.5

Those unused to mind-boggling ideas of revolting planets and high-talking scientists might be relieved to know that I can no longer fight off my fairy story temptation. So sit back and try my science-fiction version of Gaia....

There had been, once upon a time, carefree days when Pediculus and his female companion, Capitis, sunbathed and frolicked and did what was natural without a second thought. But the times they were a-changing.

The planet of Vannwick-riple was almost overrun by mini six-legged Peds and Caps, not to mention their myriad offspring. Vannwick-riplians had learned the art of reproduction only too well. The planet's pink surface and even the soaring forests — where some trees were a thousand times taller than Ped — were alive with the grey-brown sea of heaving bodies.

Ped and Cap had recently looked out on their beloved Vannwick-riple with sad, repentant eyes, knowing that they had contributed to the overcrowding. At times, the planet seemed to them to be literally 'alive', and there was the sombre thought that if their fellow Vannwick-riplians didn't try to reduce the population and the associated pollution, the planet would die.

Some extremists went even further and suggested that the planet was so alive that it would not go on tolerating such troublesome irritants. These extremists were called Pinks, and had formed themselves into an alternative political party. Meanwhile, the rest of the inhabitants, amused at the Pinks' naivety, rolled around in agonies of laughter, clasping their aching stomachs between their six legs.

'What nonsense!' they would chortle. 'Of course Vannwick-riple is just a lump of inert matter.' They said this so often that they became known as the Materialists.

'What about the Pulex problem, then?' the Pinks would counter, referring to their dreaded distant cousins. This invariably served to choke the Materialists in mid-laughter. The Pinks would always press home their advantage.

'Ever since the Pulexes started chewing up the landscape drilling for Redfood, there's been nothing but trouble and disaster!' The Pinks said this with a superior, 'better-than-them' attitude. The Pinks enjoyed their self-righteousness for, though in the past they too had drilled for Redfood, they now ate only the natural Dandruffles, small flakes of vegetation which the planet laid on its surface each day.

The Pinks, despite their irritating attitude, did have a point. The Pulexes were bad news for everybody. They were greedy, pushy and always jumping the queues of life. Some could actually leap a hundred times their own length and would often flatten more patient residents on landing. It was, however, their effect on the planet which had the others worried the most.

The Pulexes would insist on giving birth to their young on rubbish-tips, which then enlarged into pits of diseased pollution as the offspring chewed up the surrounding land. Those like Ped and Cap believed themselves to be much more civilised, simply hanging their young on the trunks of the trees. This was natural birth in harmony with the planet and its energy. The Pinks in particular liked this, because they had come to believe that they and the planet and its vegetation were all parts of one embracing force — just one vast, complex and living organism.

All this, of course, was of small significance to the Pulexes who, like their young, went in for land-eating. Their small round heads were equipped with JCB-sized teeth to pierce the planet's surface in search of the only thing that interested them — Redfood!

On many occasions this had caused horrendous planetquakes, when Vannwick-riple seemed literally to snort and then twitch from side to side before subsiding with what sounded like a deep groan. There had even been attacks from outer space in the shape of enormous, pink, fat UFOs with white razor-sharp knives for feet.

The Test-Tube Mighty Ones, the white-coated elite of Vannwick-riple, had also hinted that the planet might be living. Carbon dating tests showed that the planet was around forty years old, but other evidence contradicted this. For one thing, the height of the trees should have been much greater for a planet so old. For another, the layers of cast-off Dandruffles on the planet's surface should have been much deeper.

Could it be that Vannwick-riple was alive enough to regulate the length of its own vegetation and to periodically shampoo and clean away the dead Dandruffles from its own surface? It was an eerie thought, and one which was a taboo subject for the masses. Not for everybody, however.

'One day,' the Pinks would often predict, 'our planet will rise up against us. It will revolt against the pollution and shake us from its surface!'

Some insensitives laughed, but most preferred not to know. There came a day, however, when Ped had the last laugh. It happened the day that the planet woke up!

Rip van Winkle (the dyslexic Vannwick-riplians were always jumbling up their letters) had never had such a long nap in all his life. Why, it must be twenty years since he dropped off. As he shook the sleep from his eyes, he remembered what had roused him...that unbearable irritation in his hair. He sleepily raised his pink, long-nailed fingers which then dived down to scratch his scalp and beard until blessed relief came.

Later, after applications of appropriate lotion, anti-dandruff shampoo, a good haircut and shave, every Pediculus Capitis (louse) and every Pulex Irritans (flea) had been swept away.

Such a fate, warns Dr Lovelock, awaits planet Earth. One day it will wake from the slumber of ages and delouse itself.

Now, it all may sound like a fairy story, but we need to be fair to Dr Lovelock's hypothesis at this point. Many New Agers and scientists would readily identify with much in my little tale of planetary woe. As with our fantasy Vannwick-riple, there are strange inconsistencies on our planet. It is believed to be millions of years old and yet according to known laws of thermodynamics, earth should by now be a cold, lifeless blob of nothing floating in space. The planet's seas should also be more salty and contain tons more nickel and the atmosphere should be almost pure carbon dioxide.[6] This and other such matters have led the doctor to suggest that the living organism that is earth has the power to sustain, groom and generally look after itself.

Such inconsistencies have been an embarrassment to evolutionary scientists for years. They formed the basis of a good argument for a young earth and were used by non-evolutionary scientists to suggest a much younger planet, possibly more in line with the account of creation in the Book of Genesis.7

That, of course, was not a solution acceptable to 'positive agnostics' like Dr Lovelock. This is one reason why his hypothesis is now being seriously investigated by the New Age scientific world.

Let us now return to Findhorn. Remember Hector, the carrot-grater, and the matronly ovens called Flora, Cora and Dora? If the planet can have a name, why not a piece of metal? After all, is it not just another expression of the cosmic energy?

Even the scientists of the new physics are coming to believe that all is alive in a mysterious way. At the level of quantum physics, some strange, unscientific things are happening. When atoms are split and particles are separated, traditional rules and laws are broken, ignored and made to seem irrelevant.8

And for those who thought it idiotic to talk to plants, let us follow this New Age thinking to its logical conclusion. If metal is alive, then how much more alive are the plants? And if they are alive, then why not chat with them, encourage them, and even play them some classical music?

Once you accept planet Earth as a living being, the idea of a Harmonic Convergence affecting the planet's energies begins to make sense. This is partly the reason for the popular acceptance of yoga and Eastern meditation by people wanting to tune their inner energy to the whole planet. It has a lot to do with the increasing acceptance of New Age alternative medicine (see Appendix). Our goddess Gaia, in fact, is responsible for much in the New Age.

Actually, the ideas behind Gaia are as old as mankind's first attempts to invent a deity. Paganism and witchcraft have long bowed to Mother Earth. Gaia is Mother Earth dressed up in a scientist's white coat.

Just before continuing our Findhorn diary, perhaps a short Christian response to the concept of Gaia is in order, since it presents Christianity with a great communication bridge to New Agers.

For Gaia, read God. For Gaia shrugging off mankind, read the story of Noah's ark and the near-death of the human race (Gen 6:7,8). Gaia followers need to know that their fears for the future are in fact history, and unrepeatable history at that. A cure for their short-sightedness is all that is needed so that they can look beyond what has been created to the Almighty Creator. They can know that the Creator God has promised never again to wash mankind off the face of the earth, which is the real meaning behind the rainbow symbol they have appropriated (Gen 9:13).

In some ways, Dr Lovelock is a whole dimension away from the truth. He gives a modern scientific reason for accepting the claims of monism and pantheism that all is one and that one is God. With this, of course, we end up worshipping the creature and not the Creator, and the apostle Paul has much to say about the problems that that raises in his letter to the Romans (Rom 1:18ff).

However, in another way, Dr Lovelock is not too far from the mark when he speaks of a living planet. Many of the arguments by which he attempts to prove the existence of Gaia could just as easily be used to reveal the supreme God. In many ways, our planet is a wonderfully designed, thriving entity, constructed partly to replenish and regulate itself. James Lovelock simply stops short of recognising the planet's true Designer.

Something which is so obviously designed, like planet Earth, and indeed the universe, must logically have a Designer who is greater. Gaia is just not big enough to make the grade.

One last thought: imagine what it must be like to have as your only hope of salvation a goddess who will shrug you into oblivion if you so much as mess up her make-up! Doesn't it make you want to cry? Doesn't it make you want to reach out to your New Age neighbours and give them a hint of a God who loves them, no matter how much they mess up?

7. Firewalkers and Feminism, Talk of the Devil, and an Unjust Leap into Nature!

Monday evening

We now have the week's big news! Eileen Caddy does not normally speak to Experience Week groups but we are to be the exception. She will be with us on Thursday evening. The spirits within the group lift noticeably. Eileen obviously means much to many.

Tuesday morning

Still recovering from a hangover! It was a heady night on the beach last night. No alcohol, but plenty of incessant rhythmic dancing, much chanting to the steady, heavy beat of tom-toms, and then there were the plaintive, haunting bass notes of the drain-pipe-size didgeridoos. A Findhorn member had won the right to be community focaliser for the day, which meant that he could choose what to do (in attunement or harmony with others, one assumed). He had opted for a mad night beach party and everybody was more than willing to oblige. It was reminiscent of a Red Indian encampment, with woolly hats and boots instead of feathered head-dresses and moccasins. At moments, the evening took on the atmosphere of an earth-based, earth-worshipping, pagan gathering, which for many it was.

It was interesting for the first half-hour, but then the beat of the drums and the assorted thumps of an ever-growing percussion group began to invade the head. There was a whiff of the joss-stick and the earthy smell of warm bodies, burning drift-wood and charcoal. It was the primeval throbbing atmosphere, the heart-beat of the New Age. It echoed the Green Ecology crowd at Glastonbury Festival, or the New Age travellers resting after their annual battle with police at Stonehenge, or one of a hundred pagan, wicca or witchcraft gatherings up and down our land.

As the beach party warmed up, the circle of snake dancers weaved ever closer to the fire. Fire-jumpers dared and double-dared each other. Then somebody suggested fire-walking. A small group hived off to gossip about the last time they trod the bare coals. They had, they said, become so united with the cosmic force, their minds so dominating and controlling, their bodies so subjugated, that they were able to trip the light fantastic along the length of the smouldering bed. The stories, spliced generously with a bravado that somehow seemed at odds with the New Age concept of manhood, seemed to satisfy the group for the night. They were obviously nominal fire-walkers, lacking the commitment to do anything about it.

Traditional manhood is frowned upon within the New Age. Modern feminism — at Findhorn, quite gentle and not at all strident — has dictated increasingly that men and women move on to the same level. Now both are expected to be carers; both can be providers; together they can share their new equality. Male and female are seen as a contradiction in an age of harmony in which separation is the long way of spelling sin. New Age thinking wants everything to be of equal importance and on the same level, whether it be male or female, black or white, plant or human, animal, vegetable or mineral.

Consequently, New Age man is needing to learn how to be more feminine, developing the sensitive, compassionate and emotional side of his nature. New Age woman, on the other hand, is expected to develop her masculinity and become more assertive, ambitious and more ready to bid for power.

Christians will obviously sympathise with any attempt to change pigheaded, bigheaded and sexist modern man, but will find it difficult to agree with New Agers on how this will happen. There is a passionate belief that the New Age will bring sweeping changes to both men and women as they evolve to a higher level of consciousness. It will have to be some change, for men and women have been different ever since Adam and Eve, according to historical and social facts.

Men have always tended to be the self-centred bores, the dominant sex, the seducers, the soldiers, the bread-winners, the destructors, the violent ones. Women have generally been the opposite. Man has always been more aggressive and assertive. It was always he who went to war. Women rarely conquered new territories or battled their way to the north pole. But it was always the woman who triumphed over domestic adversity, who had victory in the family budget and controlled the 'brats' that somehow man could never manage. Now I readily admit that all this is somewhat of an overgeneralisation and that some men and some women are not in this mould. But modern writers, after two decades of feminism, are at last beginning to acknowledge that men and women are different. It is not just a matter of curves and bumps, but of the DNA genetic code. In important ways, the blueprint for making a man is different from the blueprint in a woman's genes.

Despite all this, New Agers are placing all their hopes in some indescribable, unprovable, unlikely transformation, the like of which has never happened before. It seems to be a hope without foundation.

After breakfast

Who's going to focalise the salads? Attention focuses in my direction.

'Me?' I feel a strange mixture of honour at being asked and distaste at the thought of focusing group energy.

'Well, as you can see, we're short-staffed and there's nobody else,' teases our chef-focaliser, who is still struggling with her post-holiday returning. To be honest, focalising the salads on this particular morning means doing it myself. There are just a dozen empty bowls, salad utensils and a plethora of raw vegetables to talk to and focalise. Before a decision can be reached, an extra, more experienced, pair of hands appears on the scene, and to my relief, I am demoted to the chopping-board.

How, I whimsically wonder, do my waiting victims feel? Fourteen pounds of tomatoes gaze up at the gleaming, sharp salad-knife hovering in my right hand. Even more awful, the cucumber and radish will have to look on as their red cousins are cold-bloodedly drawn and quartered, knowing that soon they will be next into the tumbrel en route to Madame Guillotine.

I suddenly chuckle wickedly, and stop just as quickly. I remember my dislike of people who caricature Christianity and then snigger at their own clever distortions, and I chide myself for doing the same to others' beliefs. And besides, the serious and sad heart of the matter surfaces in my mind as I start on the tomatoes.

All life is one and that one is God, so they believe. All life is entitled to respect, even to the point of consulting plants about their future. The community gardener had told me the previous day of having conferred with some stubborn, deep-rooted bushes. He had got them to understand the need for a move to the compost heap and they had consequently, he assured me, yielded their root-hold without a fight. The most famous Findhorn gardener, Robert Ogilvie Crombie (Roc, for short) also had similar beliefs. He and many New Agers believe that all matter has its shadow or image in an unseen etheric world, and plants are no exception. On how we should treat plants, he is recorded as saying:

> It is important to know that a plant grows within the etheric counterpart brought into existence by the Nature Spirits. By interfering with the natural growth of a plant in trying to alter the form through artificial means, often using force, man can depart from the archetypal design. Apart from the fear and pain produced in the plant, this can bring about lack of alignment with the counterpart, causing further discomfort and distress to the plant.[1]

Roc, together with Dorothy Maclean, was on daily intimate terms with the nature spirits or *devas*. Roc had a special relationship with a faun who turned out to be Pan, complete with horned head and cloven hooves.

'Well, aren't you afraid of me?' Pan had boomed out at their first meeting.

'No,' Roc had replied.

'Why not? All human beings are afraid of me. Do you know who I am?'

'Yes. I am not afraid.' Roc had explained that he felt at one with the faun and his nature subjects. On being questioned, he agreed that he loved both subjects and sovereign.

'You know, of course, that I am the devil? You have just said that you love the devil.'

Roc shook his head. He believed the oft-repeated New Age and occult stories about the church having turned all pagan gods and spirits into devils, fiends and imps.

Pan added, 'I am the servant of Almighty God, and I and my subjects are willing to come to the aid of mankind in spite of the way he has treated us and abused nature, if he affirms belief in us and asks for our help.'[2]

Roc interpreted this as an historic uniting of the nature kingdom and man. The Christian, of course, might have a slightly different interpretation, and agree with Pan's first claim!

My mind swings back to the chopping-board and the tomatoes, while at the same time recalling that a similar offer was once made to Jesus in the wilderness. Satan used the same 'if you do this, I will do that' strategem. Jesus told him where to go, for he would serve the one and only God (Mt 4:10). I also recall the biblical warnings that the devil 'masquerades as an angel of light' to mislead (2 Cor 11:14). He is the ape of God, subtle and cunning, and can catch us in his net (2 Cor 2:11; 2 Tim 2:26; 1 Tim 3:7). He is a liar and a false prophet, the god of this world, and the serpent who misled Eve in a similar garden to Roc's (2 Pet 2:1, 2 Cor 11:13; 2 Cor 4:4; Gen 3:4,5). He can also enter humans if they wish (Lk 22:3; Jn 13:27; Eph 4:27). This is an interesting warning in view of one of Roc's other statements:

> I was aware that he [Pan] was walking by my side and of a strong bond between us. He stepped behind me and then walked into me so that we became one and I saw the surroundings through his eyes...the experience was not a form of possession but of identification.[3]

Roc believed that this was 'being one with the divine', but then adds:

> The moment he stepped into me, the woods became alive with myriads of beings — elementals, nymphs, dryads, fauns, elves, gnomes, fairies — far too numerous to catalogue...
>
> I now had pipes in my hands and was aware of shaggy legs and cloven hooves. I began to dance down the path, playing the pipes.... All the nature beings were active, many dancing as they worked.[4]

This resembles Almighty God in no way. On the other hand, it is much more like the god of this world (2 Cor 4:4), another name for the devil.

On a more mundane note, if everything in the world is an expression of the life-force or energy, man being just a bigger expression than, say, the tomato, it raises some important questions:

- What right has the human to start weeding the garden?
- Why shouldn't the weeds have the same right to weed out humans?
- Shouldn't humans stop 'killing' vegetables as well as animals?
- Why don't New Agers campaign for a plant protection society equivalent to the NSPCC? Surely, if plants 'feel', New Agers should be campaigning for their rights. In view of this, to be vegetarian seems to be just as bad as being a card-carrying butcher.
- Finally, have New Agers really thought their new doctrines through to logical conclusions?

NOTE: The vast majority of New Agers certainly believe that everything is part of the life-force. Not all, however, would wish to go as far as this logical conclusion. Not all New Agers talk to plants.

Tuesday afternoon

Randolph's Leap!

It is beautiful, leafy, cool and peaceful. We stand around attuning to the forest and the quiet rush of a small waterfall nearby.

'It was here,' says our co-focaliser, Marjorie, adding some seventeenth-century date and pointing to a rocky, nine-foot stretch between river banks, 'that a Scottish chieftain called Cummings urged his horse to leap across, thereby escaping an enemy chief called Randolph.'

With this interesting titbit, we split up to commune with nature. I stay at Randolph's Leap and am immediately in harmony with the injustice of it all. Cummings risks life and limb on a death-defying leap and history names it after an enemy who chose safety first.

A bit like God and nature, I muse. God takes all the risks in creating man, gives him free-will and then, when it all goes wrong, leaps down from heaven to save mankind. Man comes along and gives all the praise to Mother Nature. It's enough to make a strong God weep. No wonder somebody once called him the chief sufferer of the universe.

I turn from Randolph's Leap. A hundred yards away, two of the group, Aussie Helen and Brigitte 'from the US of A', squat in the cross-legged Buddha pose, arms akimbo and thumbs and middle fingers joined, indicating that all life is circular. Life hasn't come from anywhere and it isn't going anywhere...the sad merry-go-round of nature.

Late afternoon

It is home time, and we gather in a wooded glade in our customary end-of-event circle.

'Who'd like to close our attunement with an appropriate word?' Terry inquires. All seem shy. No offers.

'I'll do it,' I volunteer.

'Right,' agrees Terry.

'Okay if I make it one of my own?'

'Sure. No problem.'

'Heavenly Father, thanks for everyone in this group and for your deep love for each of us.' I peep from under a half-closed lid to reassure myself that nobody has picked up any stones yet. I go for broke.

'You've given us this beautiful scenery; this lilting river; this quiet woodland, all made by your own fair hand. You are in charge of nature; you designed and created it. Thank you, Lord, for this and for giving it to us as a sign of your love. Help us to respond to you in the same way, in Jesus Christ's name. Amen.'

Silence.

Another peep. No movement. A foot nervously scuffles dead leaves across the ring. More silence. Hands are squeezed — the way we close each attunement — and we open our eyes. One or two glances flicker across mine but pretend they didn't.

'That was beautiful!' This comes from Christina, the ex-Roman Catholic. I could hug her.

'Great, Kev!' That's down-under Richard, swinging an arm in my direction as though tossing a boomerang. 'Thanks.'

Suddenly, we're all walking back to the bus, cheerful, accepting and tolerant. If some are into God as a Father, no problem; they want to pray in Jesus' name, fine; they want to give God the glory instead of Gaia, it's okay. Live and let live. Let's all be one happy family. Harmony is the name of the game.

Truth is a minor casualty.

8. Business — New Age Style

Wednesday

I skip the muesli and figs this morning and opt for the prunes and dates. Brigitte is already at the breakfast-table, glowing after her dawn-time hour of meditation on the tor above the community.

'I can hardly wait 'til tomorrow.' In her excitement her North American accent is tinted with mid-European echoes, betraying her German roots. Not being a morning person, I manage to raise an inquiring eyebrow in her direction as I meditate on my first prune.

'Eileen Caddy!' enthuses Brigitte. 'She's with us tomorrow night.'

I smile and stifle a sudden urge to shake some sense into her. My grumpiness in part comes from the early hour of the day. ('He's not a Christian until nine o'clock in the morning,' runs the family joke at our house.) But I am also irked by Brigitte's naivety. Her whole life rests on intuition. Why, oh, why, are people becoming so gullible today? A silver-haired matron called Eileen claims that God has spoken to her in a remote Scottish fishing village, she writes a couple of books, does a European tour or two, and suddenly Brigitte and thousands of others are jetting in from all corners of the world to sit before the latest guru. And yet Brigitte is by no means simple. Her education is to university standard, her travel is worldwide and her experience and common sense in everyday areas is obvious.

I catch sight of the group on the next table. It reinforces the fact that my fellow community members are no strangers to intelligence. It strikes me, not for the first time, that I am surrounded by thoughtful, discerning, mainly middle-class people whose lives are not what they want them to be. Bright people yearning to be beautiful people.

Peter nods as our glances connect over Brigitte's left shoulder. He is a Swiss business consultant with a clientele ranged across Europe and he is here with his colleagues from five other countries, partly to study how New Age philosophies can boost commerce and industry in the European Economic Community. The main theme of their symposium is transformation of organisations and how to manage change at the levels of the individual, the company, Europe, and even at a global level. This is an offshoot of a series of international symposia which began in the United States in 1983.

We had spent an hour the previous evening discussing change and transformation, the nub of the New Age. I had wanted to know of the New Age involvement in the world's market-place, and how it intended to cope with their nasty J.R. Ewing characters. How was the City of corruption and collusion going to be transformed come the New Age? Our conversation went something like this:

Q. Seeing what Findhorn represents and offers, do you feel it can benefit our captains of industry, commerce and business?

A. Yes, I think that managers would profit from just being here. It can shape a certain part of themselves which even within training programmes is not handled so easily as by just coming here and being here. Perspectives open up here that are difficult elsewhere.

Q. A spiritual dimension?

A. Yes…a spiritual festival, a whole different perspective on business and what we are doing with business…the role of relationships…how they are being handled. It is such a different context…you can go back into the City with new eyes.

Q. Does Findhorn have something realistic to contribute in controlling business and the businessman?

A. For me, the essence of business is exchange. This is what business is about, not a fixation on pure profit and short-term gain. It is about human exchange. It is a human relationship that is being enacted.

Q. But what about the grabber, the one who's more concerned about profit than people?

A. That is where business has got lost. It's actually bad business. It may look good in the short term, but it's bad. In terms of human relationships, you are actually creating pain to someone and also to yourself.

Q. What do you feel is the solution — re-education?

A. Yes. This opening of self is occurring whether you like it or not. As you open, you discover more opportunities emerging because you become more skilful. On the other hand, you find certain avenues closing off…it becomes impossible for me to conclude a transaction which isn't working for me and for somebody else. Finding the one avenue that does work is worth so much more. It's worth everything.

Q. But there are still the rip off merchants. What do you do with them?

A. Yes, they are there. I don't think there's very much to do, to tell you the truth. Eileen Caddy talks a lot about loving them. I think we each have our own paths — I used to be one of those on the other path until I got to the place where it was too painful. Pain exists for everybody who is on that other path.

But how are the J.R. Ewings who thrive on pain going to be changed for the New Age? This was a question I put not only to Peter and Findhorn, but to the rest of the New Age in general research questions. The following are some of the answers.

Intuitive leadership

A £375 week's course on how to help leaders 'follow those inward directions being whispered to us'. The course promises to address the multidimensional role of leader in a 'co-creative gathering, where we will open ourselves to inner listening and outer dialogue, with [Findhorn] Foundation faculty and leaders from different fields'.[1] This prompts another question: what is the source of the inner guidance our leaders will receive? The answers are as many as there are New Agers. Everybody has his or her own idea. The most popularly held concept is of an inner divinity, the local form of the life-force in action.

For consultants and managers

A £325 working retreat. In addition to relaxation and reflection with their peers, leaders can refresh 'body, mind and spirit'. Specific topics may include meditation, intuitive development and bodywork (various techniques to remove past traumas which, it is claimed, cause blocks to the flow of energy in the body). We are not told the identity of the energy.[2]

Transformation game

'A remarkable new way to experience and express your deepest self — it gives you what you ask for…a sensitive and insightful tool to enable deep change to occur.' It costs £35.50 in its board-game form but for ten times the amount you can join the life-size version. The Planetary Game, with up to a hundred fellow-players. Its stated aim is to bring

> clarity, insight and healing to areas of planetary and personal concern…. It requires us to expand our openness to the moving and purposeful presence of the spirit, and to engage fully with our potential to effect planetary changes, as we respond to the challenges and opportunities of this time on earth.

The course in miracles

Hundreds of thousands, especially businessmen and industrialists, claim to have been profoundly affected and given a new lease of spiritual life through this course. Not many of them realise that it is a channelled course, which means the text came through inner dictation from a spirit guide. American psychologists Drs Helen Schucman and William N. Thetford misleadingly presented the finished course in Christian language in 1975. It encourages contact with the 'voice of inner wisdom' (love) and identifies 'the voice of the ego' (fear). Findhorn's Path of Forgiveness version uses 'meditation, guided imagery and higher-self exercises' to help participants 'contact the Holy Spirit within' (cost up to £290).

And elsewhere in the New Age…

Esalen Institute

Early in the hippy sixties of California, Richard Price and Michael Murphy pioneered and developed a large range of techniques and ideas in personal growth and started the institute. This became the world inspiration for the Human Potential Movement and humanistic psychology, based on the idea that man has all that he needs within himself.

The Forum

Thousands of our leaders have gone through this or associated groups like Breakthrough Foundation, Centres Network, Education Network, Holiday Project and Hunger Project. They are all based on Werner Erhard Associates and Erhard Seminars Training (known as 'est'), founded by Erhard at the beginning of the seventies. Est became infamous for verbal batterings and high-powered emotional attacks, designed to force change on its willing victims, mainly management trainees, in its course called The Training. Gradually, this was adjusted into a more civilised technique and was renamed The Forum (or one of the other names depending on suitability). It is based on spiritually empowering individuals to be what they wish to be. The identity of the power is not named, though the teachings are based on the 'oneness of the universe', the concept which underlies monism and pantheism.

Designer and writer Chris Bourne, who has spent a decade researching New Age manifestations, went to an introductory evening and was finally invited to pay the £350 joining fee. He declined, and when his trainer asked for his reason, he replied:

> Because you cannot tell me the source of your empowerment. I will not submit myself to any power which does not have a name and if you think this does not matter, it is you and not I who do not understand the nature of what you are doing.[3]

Writing in *21st Century Christian* magazine, Chris, a member of the Cobham Fellowship and Pioneer Team, added:

> I do not believe that the source of the power is particularly difficult to identify or even that it is the only issue at stake. Now, I don't mean by this that I am dismissing rather superficially the power as being simply demonic. What I mean is that, as a New Age phenomenon, est should have been better understood by that trainer. She should have known that the power was supposed to be her own divinity, a tapping in to 'oneness', the executive energy of the universe.[4]

Transcendental Meditation

A TM industrial village has now been constructed in Skelmersdale New Town, Lancashire, where workers are encouraged to take two twenty-minute meditation breaks each shift. It is part of the 'Maharishi effect', the theory that an industry, or a community, or the surrounding area will be changed for the better if one per cent of the population meditates. It will provide good vibrations which will beneficially affect everybody. TM, the teaching of Maharishi Mahesh Yogi, involves chanting mantras, the names of fourth-class Hindu gods. At the advanced TM-Sidhi Programme levels, psychic powers are added, such as levitation, extra-sensory perception, telepathy, telekinesis, spiritual healing and control of mind over body.

TM preaches salvation through Eastern techniques of meditation, and as such qualifies as 'another gospel' in the eyes of Christianity.[5] Some leaders in the Christian church are not helping by their promotion of this 'other gospel' in *TM: An Aid to Christian Growth*.[6] This book, reprinted by popular demand, is made up of contributions from Roman Catholic priests and TM teachers who seek (unsuccessfully) to harmonise the Maharishi method and Christianity.

Neuro-linguistic programming

This is one of the fastest growing offshoots of applied humanistic psychology and has wide applications in business, as well as in education and personal development. This again is based on man delving into his own psyche and self to find answers. It is a hybrid of hypnotherapy, family therapy and Gestalt therapy. Fritz Perls gained a worldwide reputation by using Gestalt — a therapy which aims to put the client in contact with him/herself and the world — at Esalen Institute. All that matters, said Perls, was the here and now; not the past, nor the future, just the living moment and feeling good and complete about it. Good positive thinking based solely on human endeavours.

Pathworking

This is a new technique for businessmen and the general public, even though it can be traced back to the occult magic of the earliest Egyptian, Sumerian and Chaldean civilisations. It was under wraps, known only to esoteric societies until one of their number, occultist Dolores Ashcroft-Nowicki, decided that it was essential for a dawning New Age to understand the mental doorways or paths between the known and unknown and between the physical and the non-physical. Pathworking is based on the ancient occultic Qabalistic Tree of Life and employs 'guided meditation' through channelled spirits. Not recommended for those who like to retain a balanced boardroom sanity.

Silva mind-control

This has a significant following in the West, especially among leaders who are attracted by promises of improved memory, higher IQ and an increased learning speed. The followers of the Silva Method (as it is now increasingly becoming known) also claim that it develops telepathy. In some ways, Texas-born Jose Silva's mind-control programme was taken from occult pathworking and also from visualisation techniques which involve picturing what you want. Visualisation is at the heart of all occult practice in modern witchcraft and satanism. It is the first principle learned in casting spells and charms. You form the picture and then throw it into the ether to do its work. See it, be it. Name it, claim it. Think it, create it. It can create problems when your works manager is doing the same thing in his office.

Those who are quick will have already recognised the Christian version of Silva mind-control. The American Christian 'name it, claim it' clan lifted the whole idea from Silva's secular humanism. Faith became not so much a gift from God as something within for us to exercise. Faith worked simply by announcing what you wanted then positively going for it. The occult dressed as an angel of light....

Psychovisual therapy

'Stress! Today's killer! Don't be a worrier — be a warrior.' So runs an advertisement from television's Stuart Hall, one of innumerable newspaper blurbs offering videos to help people find their inner self, combat stress, relax, and turn problems into challenges.[7] Self-help 'will never be easier' promises another company, New World, which offers video hypnosis for ultimate relaxation, incredible self-confidence, developing psychic ability, positive thinking and a boost to brain power. It is all done through subliminal messages and is 'the most powerful brain/mind programming in the world'.[8]

Lifestyle Libraries offer a 'therapist in a cupboard' once you've taken home one of their psychovisual tapes, 'a potent, self-development multi-system' combined with the 'awesome power brought forward from the subconscious mind by subliminal suggestion'.[9]

Yoga

Keep-fit, lessen-stress hatha is the form of yoga mainly practised in Britain, due in great part to television coverage by exponents like Richard Hittleman. This gentleman introduced his viewers to the idea that

> all life is sustained by a force which the yogis have
> named *prana* (breath or life-force)...all living things
> must receive the life-force to sustain themselves....
> The more life-force, the more awareness of life and all
> its implications; the less life-force, the less sense of
> life and the realisation of its meaning and purpose.[10]

This is supposed to be the acceptable face of a Hindu philosophy of self-discipline and worship. Other forms of yoga (a Sanskrit word meaning 'union' with the force) are rapidly being accepted. There is Dhyana, involving trance states; Jnana, with a knowledge of esoteric doctrines of the Hindu sacred books, the Vedas; Kundalini, arousing the serpent force curled round the base of the spine; Laya, used widely in Western magical systems to activate the chakras (energy points) of the body; Mantra, driving the mind to higher things through sound; and Raja, the king of yoga which, it is claimed, leads to full enlightenment.

Zen Buddhism

Britain went through a phase when the menu of life offered Zen with everything. You could even discover 'Zen and Motor-cycle Repairs'. Zen sets out to shatter cosy ritualistic performances or lives which are set in deep ruts, whether in business or home life. Disciples are prised loose from old habits by shock tactics. One Zen master had the habit of answering his students' deep questions by whacking them round the ear with a stick. It made them think. This, however, is not recommended on the modern shop-floor. Zen has developed more subtle approaches for Britain.

Zone therapy

With this, the forty-year-old businessman 'can look and feel ten years younger', boasts Joseph Corvo, who has been practising zone therapy for more than thirty years. He claims royal princess patronage and also has a number of celebrity clients, according to his book on the subject.[11] Actor Michael York states, 'I have discovered extraordinary healers around the world, and even when you shake their hands you're aware of a power. I feel that in Joseph Corvo.'[12]

Zone therapy was actually the brainchild of an American doctor, William Fitzgerald, who was testing oriental therapies for effectiveness. He experimented with the idea that the body was divided into various zones, the first two zones, for instance, stretching from the top of the head to the forehead and into the thumbs and big toes.

If business is a bit mind-blowing or the boardroom becomes too stressful, you simply whip off a shoe and massage your big toe.

Whatever your problem in business, or elsewhere for that matter, the forces of nature or the power within yourself can provide a solution. That is the claim of all these courses, and many more besides. Nothing to do with God, of course! Who needs a deity when you can just plug into the energies of the earth or the body?

The bright people might not be so clever after all.

'You fool!' said God one day to an agricultural magnate planning to expand into the building business, a man who trusted in the earth's energies and his own resources.

'You fool! This very night your life will be demanded from you. Then who will get what you have prepared for yourself? This is how it will be with anyone who stores up things for himself but is not rich towards God' (Lk 12:20 – 21).

Those following the above systems are fools not only because they omit God, but also because they lose touch with reality. The 'get up and go for it' mentality is fine for a fine day. But what happens when a person is flat on his back and he cannot even get up to go anywhere? What happens when his puny power packs up and he has nobody but himself to rely on? His back may have gone! Burn-out may have struck! A hundred and one other disabilities may have crippled him. Does he have to keep on playing the charade for ever? When can he be allowed to come to his senses and realise that God never meant him to go solo for life?

Before this book reached the publisher, it was test-read by a dozen critics. My former parish licensed reader, Margaret, exploded in Biro at this point in the original manuscript.

'Just what is the Christian church doing? All these people believe whole-heartedly that they can plug into a spiritual or inner power, while the majority in our church believe the spiritual and its power died long ago, about the time the Bible was written. The power was there for the first Christians but not for us today. Some believe it was never present at all.

'Why isn't the Christian church giving an alternative to the New Age? Why don't we, for instance, run our own relaxation and meditation classes to counter the stress of modern living? Why are we leaving all this to the non-Christians?'

Are any readers out there noting this? Maybe that's the subject for another book: how to run a safe, biblical anti-stress school that builds up people in a positive way. Christian positive thinking should certainly be included.

Margaret, often in the past an anxiety victim, stressed, 'It is only God's power through a Christian version of positive thinking that's helped me survive.'

And she's right, and biblical!

The Christian packs the power of God within and the Lord can do immeasurably more than all we can ask (Eph 3:20). God's real wise men in the Book of Proverbs tell us to think positively. It's non-stop feasting for the cheerful but abject wretchedness for the negative and oppressed (15:15). Whatever a man is inside, that will he be on the outside (23:7). Positively go for the best and life will go in that direction (21:21). Be purposeful and understand where you need to go (20:5). Go for good and you will find it (11:27).

I am often asked how I can minister within paganism and the occult and the New Age without getting fearful. The answer is that I do get frightened, but the fear is more often than not under the firm control of a God-given faith. The Lord has graciously taught me a very simple truth: there is nothing that the devil or his forces can do to me without God's permission. And if God allows it, then that's okay. It will be for my good in the end. The proof of that is in the Book of Job and in promises such as Romans 8:28: 'In all things God works for the good of those who love him.' In other words, whichever way life goes, I'm the winner, because ultimately I am on the winning side. Thank God for his positive thinking.

Human positive thinking will never fully cope with our fears and inadequacies. It is, after all, merely personal play-acting. It is as shy and retiring as the flower at sunset. Come the dark, it closes up and shrinks. Come the valleys and pits of life, positive thinking can only collapse in on itself.

The positive thinking based on God and his word is strong enough even to take us through the valley of the shadow of death. And there is nothing stronger than that.

At times, during my week at Findhorn and since, I have been saddened by the naivety of bright people using any gullible recipe to try to make themselves beautiful people. Surely, the New Age has got more to offer than misleading, mind-bending courses? There must be more to it than contacting some unidentified inner wisdom which so far man has kept remarkably well hidden?

Just what is the New Age recipe for producing New Age man?

9. Salvation by Faith in…
a Tidal Wave of Love, or
the Hundredth Monkey

Still Wednesday

Jenny has joined us for breakfast; Jenny the single
mum from London, the honest one who stands no
nonsense. We talk about realism; about street riots
and the hopeless poverty traps in the hidden parts of our
cities and housing estates; about the rich getting richer,
the poor getting angrier.

Jenny sees more clearly than others in the group. Like
many who have spent time in the New Age scene, she
feels able to question and challenge, for there is a basic
honesty among New Agers. For instance, places like
Findhorn understand that they are attracting many of the
middle class and the thinkers, but few from areas of
deprivation. The New Agers enjoy their sacred dancing,
the leafy glades of Randolph's Leap and the assorted
mind-stretching exercises, but they struggle when faced
with the hard realities of the human condition.

New Zealander Tom, hearing our conversation from
the adjoining breakfast-table, leans over to join in. Tom is
nobody's fool. He has shared some of himself so far this
week but mostly he has just listened and looked on.
When he does open up, it is always with a sharp edge,
using words like spades to get to what is solid. There have

already been one or two things he has questioned. Tom still remains unconvinced about the so-called 'love' or 'inner energy' promoted by Findhorn, and is outwardly sceptical when faced with the array of human potential training courses. In a hard twenty-eight years, he has experienced life in its dirty underwear. He has emerged from a scarred, abused childhood with an Aussie dad who brushed aside emotion and Tom as irrelevant. Tom now wanders an empty world, needing as he has previously admitted in an unguarded moment of softness, to be filled with a love he has yet to discover.

The New Age promises humanity much, but can it deliver? Can it save people from their own weaknesses and stupidity?

Already, we have focused on one suggested answer — the est-forum type of do-it-yourself improvement, the Human Potential Movement. This is man trying to pull himself up by his own bootlaces, with all the impossibilities which that picture conjures up. Before his conversion, the apostle Paul devoted all his energy to trying to do just that as a good, law-abiding Jew, and he failed miserably. He described the process in his letter to the Romans: 'I do not understand what I do. For what I want to do I do not do, but what I hate I do' (Rom 7:15).

Man cannot lift himself up to God. A law of gravity operates in the spiritual realm just as forcefully as in the physical. So what other methods of salvation are on offer in the New Age?

Similarly to Christianity, the New Age offers salvation by faith — not, of course, in Jesus Christ and his completed work of dying for our sins on the cross of Calvary. New Age salvation comes by faith in one of the following:

A tidal wave of love

Sir George Trevelyan, a frequent visitor to Findhorn, who leads his own Wrekin Trust in Malvern and who is known as the father of the New Age, explains:

> The phenomenon of our age is that into the earth there is now seeping and flooding a rising tide of sheer love. This is the real Second Coming...The Christ [not Jesus, but the cosmic Christ power as seen in various religious leaders] is coming...Not incarnating in a particular body as with Jesus but into every one of us who creates the stilled centre, having disposed of anger and fear and criticism and doubt and all that. We create a vacuum into which this rising tide of love can seep and flood. Don't believe it, but watch it. Think it. I have no doubt whatever that this is really happening, and it is the most exciting thing. It is the true purpose of our age.[1]

After Sir George, who once tutored Prince Philip at Gordonstoun, had finished one of his lectures one evening, I asked him what would happen to those who refused to open themselves up to the cosmic love. He firmly announced, 'They will be lifted away to another planet and another life to be re-educated.'

As Sir George said this, he stood before the Communion table of St James' Anglican Church in Piccadilly, London. It did not seem to matter that the nearby church Bible stated that man had only one life to live, after which came death and judgement (Heb 9:27). He bypassed the truth that there was only one way to God through the one Christ Jesus (Jn 14:6). Sir George did not seem to have heard of the promise that Jesus would come back in a body, just as the disciples had seen him go (Acts 1:11).

But what he must have known about, and chose to

leave to one side, was the rising tide of hate and anger that was seeping and flooding into at least forty war zones around the world as he lectured. A little after he spoke, the figure went up to forty-one, as President Saddam Hussein of Iraq invaded Kuwait. Had Sir George not stopped to wonder about the absence of a rising tide of love in South Africa the day before his talk, when 500 died in a tidal wave of hate in the black townships? And what of the corruption that still leaves two thirds of the world hungry?

Some in the New Age counter this argument with the 'wave of love' that has swept away the Iron Curtain, or the wave of aid to Ethiopia, and the overwhelming concern about the planet and its future. Every one of us would be delighted if these were authentic signs of true change in man. Realistically, the most that can be stated is that though humans made in God's image produce love and goodness, humans remade in their own sinful images also send out the tidal waves of hate. These waves ebb and flow across the various scenes of life, and will continue to do so until the return of Jesus Christ. (See Mark chapter 13, especially verses 7 and 8.)

Sir George, a lovable grandfather-figure with immense spiritual dignity and very approachable, is a typical New Age optimist. There are many of them, for he has been their 'father' for the last couple of decades. He unrealistically gives too much goodness to humanity and overlooks the inherent evil streak, although there are those in the New Age who see this clearly.

Dr William Bloom, the organiser of Alternatives, the New Age centre based at St James', Piccadilly, London, explained to me, 'The language of Christian tradition which talks about sinfulness is one that not a lot of New Agers can accept.'

Dr Bloom, who tries to fulfil a go-between role with

respect to Christianity and the New Age, believes that both sides should talk about the 'shadow side of man'. This is caused, he says, by 'man's own essential materialism', because he rejects his spirituality and also God.

'And I would want to say in New Age terms,' he continues, 'that what is required to redeem that state is a surrender to Christ, but I might not use the word "Christ" — perhaps surrender to unconditional love.'

In this statement, Dr Bloom hints at his own New Age solution to man's salvation, and we come back to this later.

In the meantime, we shall go on to consider another New Age hope for mankind. This time it is salvation by faith in:

The Hundredth Monkey

This is a favourite in the New Age.

Once upon a time, a monkey was put in a cage and couldn't escape. A second, then a third, then a fourth monkey also went into the cage, but still no escape. It wasn't until the hundredth monkey was put in, that the cage eventually burst under the pressure, and all the occupants escaped.

The moral of the tale is that when the number of 'renewed' humans reaches a certain critical level, then the bonds of the old age will no longer be able to hold back the human race. They will break out to evolve on to a new and higher level of consciousness.

This is not the original Hundredth Monkey tale as outlined in Lyall Watson's works, but it seems to be the popular New Age version. New Agers take this old folk-tale a step further. When sufficient humans know of the New Age, then the information will spread like wildfire, rather like the blue tits and the milk bottles in the fifties.

Scientists began to study the strange action of a small number of tits in Britain which learned to siphon off cream after pecking through silver-foil tops on milk bottles. Within three years, the habit had spread throughout Europe's population of blue tits. Scientist Rupert Sheldrake christened the phenomenon 'morphic resonance' — information reverberating through one form or species. Tests on rats, birds and children have since provided additional evidence, but it is far from conclusive. Sheldrake gave a now famous definition of morphic resonance:

> If rats are taught a new trick in Manchester, then rats of the same breed all over the world should show a tendency to learn the trick more rapidly, even in the absence of any known type of physical connection or communication.

Don't dismiss morphic resonance or the Hundredth Monkey idea too lightly. New Agers certainly do not. And it is true that there may be methods of communication of which we are still ignorant. The mind, both of animals and humans, is still largely virgin territory, waiting for more explorers to venture even further into our dark interiors. We need also to consider the mighty power of peer group pressure. If enough of our friends, neighbours or work-mates believe something, it takes a strong-willed person to resist the temptation to fall in line. If sufficient lead is given, man will follow, whether it be Nazi Germany, Jim Jones and the Jonestown suicides, or our teenagers who get 'mixed up with that bad lot down the road'.

Perhaps faith in the Hundredth Monkey might not be as daft as it first seems. Maybe this can bring salvation for man. There are, however, one or two problems.

People are not blue tits. Nor are they rats, though they

may behave like them sometimes. Human beings are not often at the whim of the majority. They rarely, if ever, behave like lemmings, which reach a critical number and then throw themselves into the sea. On the thankfully rare occasions when mass hysteria does make men and women flock as one, it is almost always in a downward and evil direction: lynch mobs, Nazi Germany, street and soccer terrace riots. Occasionally, we find a religious revival or an Ethiopian appeal creating a significant human tide of good. But human sin ensures that the condition is temporary.

In normal times, people are governed by their own desires and needs. Altruism is present but easily brushed aside. Realistically, we are centred on self, not the desires and needs of others. We want to be gods and we are loath to let others rule our lives, though reluctantly we let this happen at times out of fear or need. The Bible describes the condition as sin.

Many have tried to bring in new ages in history, but the rise of every empire inevitably has been followed by a fall. There has always been somebody greater and bigger, with other ideas, around the corners of time. Humanity has never been swayed totally in one direction in the whole of history. Even when the world reached its nadir, there was Noah and his family who, by the grace of God, refused to be swept away in a flood of sin.

It is interesting to note that morphic resonance and the Hundredth Monkey principle dramatically failed at the very time they should have succeeded. A new age began after the ark landed on Mount Ararat. The new world's whole population of eight people followed God and loved him. So how come it did not stop that way when family, social and world pressures all drove man to God? If the Hundredth Monkey theory worked, this is the way it should have stayed.

It could be that in the next few years a wave of sweetness and light might sweep people towards a seeming New Age. But it will last only as long as man's selfishness allows.

There are two more New Age hopes for man's salvation and these need fuller treatment, for they present a much greater threat to the truth.

10. Salvation by Faith in...
the Cosmic Christ

Wednesday evening

'Are you telling us we're all wrong?' Blunt New Zealander Tom eventually hits on the one question I have been half dreading, half wanting since the week started.

'You reckon,' continues Tom, with a tone and expression reflecting a mixture of amusement, indignation and disbelief, 'that your Jesus really is the only way and we're on the wrong road and heading in the opposite direction?'

I quietly return Tom's steady look.

All in the group are doing what is right in their own eyes. The fact that some of their beliefs directly contradict those of others is not important. What matters, as they are fond of repeating, is that 'It's right for me, at this time, in this culture, and in this life; it may not be right for me next year, but it's okay now.' Here is the relativism of our anything-goes age summed up in a thought. No absolutes, no clear-cut right or wrong, no particular way — only a non-stick Teflon truth...and especially, no special outstanding life to follow. There are many god-men or gurus, innumerable roads, countless truths and a

Pantheon of gods. Here is the third hope of the New Age: salvation by faith in...

The Christ figure

Such a figure is said to be the essence of deity, which arises throughout history in different generations and within various cultures. Such a god-man is given as an example to follow; to be light shining in the darkness of human suffering.

That I should sit in a New Age group and have the audacity to insist that this figure came only once, and for all generations and cultures, is New Age heresy!

Tom and the rest of the group still wait for my answer.

In my second-day testimony, I had spoken of finding the truth. They had thought then that that was 'fine for me'. Without being pushy, and in response to questions, I had occasionally repeated in a variety of forms that Jesus was 'the way, the truth and the life' and that there was no other way to God. Just before Tom's question, one of the group had suggested that Jesus was 'one expression of the cosmic Christ consciousness'. I had gently reminded the group that Jesus would have disagreed with them. He was rather narrow-minded and quite intolerant of those who preached another message, for he claimed to be the only way.

Tom's question hangs in the air. Do I really think that they are all wrong?

My mind is working fast to find an answer that will not offend and yet still be truthful. At last, the only appropriate response comes to the lips...

'Yes.'

Irritation vibrates through the sanctuary in which we are gathered. Our attunement jangles with this off-key note. No amused smiles now.

'I'm glad I can say this knowing that you will accept it,'

I half suggest, hoping they don't catch the quaver in my voice. Actually, they have little alternative but to accept it if they are as liberal as they pretend.

'You believe that everybody has the right to their own truth,' I continue, with a little more boldness, 'and you believe that we have to accept each other's truths no matter what they might be. If I am to follow Jesus Christ, then I have to say that he's right and you are wrong. I also believe that this is not my truth and only okay for me. It is *the* truth and it applies to you.'

Silence.

The unwritten rule of the group stands. Each should accept everything without comment or criticism. The group are thinking that I am a narrow-minded pain in the neck, but our agreed ritual will not permit them to express it. I am safe — at least until the group ends.

Every Christian worth his witness will be alongside me so far in this chapter. Each of you meets this same issue every time you stand up for Jesus in a world where people are fanatically against fanatics. Our liberal age is anything but liberal. The uniqueness of Jesus Christ is the number one issue facing Christians today in our multifaith, multicultural age of relativism.

The New Age's solution to a 'multi' society is a multi-Christ — a Christ for all seasons, shades and sects, and woe betide any who stand against it.

Our group ends with an early, uneasy attunement and I find myself walking alone to the lounge for evening coffee. Now there are no rituals, and no holds barred. Quietly but firmly at first, they attempt to show me the error of my ways. I quietly insist that, if I am to be true to Jesus, I have to accept him as the only way. The responses become louder.

'You cannot seriously expect us to take that!'

'Who are you to say that you are right and I am wrong?'

'What's so special about your almighty Jesus?'

'The New Age stands no chance with fanatics like you.'

'Explain yourself…'

The ensuing discussion-cum-argument rages for an hour, orchestrated by musicians Graham and Susan.

I feel as we talk that this is the week's crossroad. This is the last time I'm going to be part of the group. From now on, eyes are not going to meet mine, except by accident. Smiles are going to be tight and artificial. I have overstepped the accepted mark and though most of the international company don't know where it is or what it means, I'm going to be sent to Coventry.

To believe in only one way and one truth at the dawning of a New Age is just not acceptable.

Even the Christian church is struggling with the status of Jesus in the face of other faiths. In some parts of our church, the Son of God is almost demoted to an also-ran among religious leaders. Some groups and even cathedrals have difficulty even squeezing Jesus Christ into the events they sponsor. One multifaith service in Canterbury Cathedral missed out Jesus altogether.[1]

In other areas, Jesus is merged with the cosmic Christ figure and becomes totally mixed up with almost every other religious leader in history. Leading the way in this is the New Age centre, Alternatives, based at St James', Piccadilly.

Dr William Bloom, a co-director of Alternatives, is the sincere and charming go-between who, as we have already noted, seeks where possible to harmonise Christianity, 'the sacred tradition he loves', and the New Age. To this end, he has written several books, one of which is described as '*the* meditation book' for the movement. He has also written on ley lines, devas, fairies and angels. His most recent book presents 'a new approach to festivals' like 'new moons, full moons, solstices, equinoxes, fire festivals', giving 'ideas to help you understand and work them'.[2]

Dr Bloom was able to help me understand the New Age hope in the Christ consciousness, or 'Christ figure' as he called it. He began with his approach to the Christian Scriptures: 'The Bible for me is an expression of deity, but God manifests in different forms through different cultures in different historical periods, and if I was to give the Bible exclusive place as an interpretation of reality, then I would be marginalising the profound and wonderful holy scriptures of other world religions. I don't think I can do that. What I can do is to say that God manifests through these cultures, through the Bhagavad Gita [best known of Hindu scriptures], through the Qur'an and through the Bible.'[3]

Dr Bloom had a non-church upbringing and, as an adult, was brought into 'a direct experience' of 'the love, compassion and grace of God', through a 'series of personal revelatory experiences', and 'there was an element within all that that I recognised as Christ'. As he went on to share, pray and meditate with others of different faiths, he found that they too had had similar experiences through Hinduism's Krishna or one of the Buddhas.

'But it is Christ, speaking to different cultures through different forms,' said Dr Bloom. 'The Christ is manifest everywhere to people on the planet and they do not need to have heard the word "Jesus" in order to have experienced Christ. The Christ died for us on the cross and rose again, and that spirit permeated the whole of the planet, and people were touched by it, whether or not they had ever heard the words of the gospel.'

But what, I enquired, of Jesus' claim, 'I am the way, the truth and the life. No one comes to the Father except through me' (Jn 14:6)?

Dr Bloom translates this as Jesus being 'a model one hundred per cent appropriate for his culture. If he were in a different culture at a different time, he would maybe require a different colouring.' He accepts that the 'christing of Jesus was unique', but only in the sense that there was only one Jesus 'christed'.

Mankind, he maintains, has been provided by God with 'a *smörgåsbord* of approaches' to salvation, but 'it comes down to one element, which is people opening their hearts to Christ, and letting Christ incarnate fully into them'. Not necessarily Jesus Christ, of course. Dr Bloom accepts that Jesus Christ died for him on the cross, but cannot accept that Christ's death is sufficient for his salvation. His own personal model of salvation therefore adds reincarnation, as do many Christian-based New Agers. We shall deal with reincarnation later.

Nobody would pretend that go-between roles are easy, and especially between Christianity and the New Age. Dr Bloom has done well to play a balanced role between the movement and the modern liberal version of Christianity. However, when set against the more biblical demands of traditional, orthodox Christianity, Dr Bloom has not been as successful.

When Jesus said, 'I am the way,' he was not only revealing the way, he *was* the way. He was the Saviour. Jesus was claiming that he alone was the food of life, the gateway of salvation, the access to the Father (Jn 6:35; 10:9; Eph 2:18). Only his blood was the way to God's Holy Place, not the Buddha's, nor Krishna's. Jesus claimed to be the one and only Son. Only belief in him was the way to eternal life. There was no other name under the sun by which man could be saved (Heb 10:19,20; Jn 3:14ff; Acts 4:12).

Jesus said he was 'the truth'. Nobody else. If somebody else is the truth, then Jesus cannot be the truth. Buddha claimed there was no God. Jesus claimed to be the Son of God. Muhammad said that God had no son.

If the Christ figure has come in all three, as Dr Bloom and many others claim, then he is not making a very good job of the truth. In fact, it is very difficult to see what attracts people to this dithering, deceived and deceiving Christ figure.

Just suppose for a moment that this Christ figure was real. What use would he be to us, when he cannot make up his mind from one generation to the next and from one culture to another? This New Age Christ figure needs a Saviour himself!

As for Jesus, the Bible says of him: 'The Word [God] became flesh, and made his dwelling [one dwelling, not many in various cultures and at various times] among us' (Jn 1:14).

If Christ had already incarnated on earth as the Buddha or Krishna and was coming again as Muhammad, not to mention thirty-odd other fleeting appearances for minor tribal sects, why did he claim to be the only one, and warn his disciples to beware of imitations (Mt 24:4,5)?

Jesus said he was 'the life'. When Prince Siddhartha Gautama, the one generally known as 'the Buddha', died at the age of eighty around 483 BC, he was put in a tomb and he stayed there. Muhammad was sixty-two when his health failed and he was buried in Medina in 632 AD. His body is there today. It is the same story with every other hint of a Christ figure — except Jesus.

Jesus Christ is 'the life' because only he has beaten death through the Resurrection, and through him we shall all have life. He is not just an example of life, like the other so-called Christ figures. He is the One who actually is the life. 'Through him were all things made; without him nothing was made that has been made. In him was life, and that life was the light of men' (Jn 1:3,4; cf 11:25).

Those who carelessly merge religions regardless of what truth is, and disregard any insults and offence they may give to the individual religions, should consider the following facts.

The Buddha never claimed to be the way or the saviour, but merely a guide to the nothingness of nirvana. For much of his life, the Buddha proved to be a false way, misleading the early wandering holy men into rigorous fasting. He started to eat again and retreated into meditation under a bo tree. Eventually, he proposed the Middle Way between rich living and asceticism which he believed eventually ran to a bliss of nothingness. At no time did he ever claim to be the way himself. The Buddha's way has been further eroded by his followers breaking into various contradictory schools of Buddhism: Mahayana; Theravada; and Zen, a hybrid of the first two.

The Hindu god-men, Krishna and Rama, the avatars or incarnations of Vishnu, are contradictory Christ figures. Rama was benevolent and Krishna was a rather impetuous, violent and erotic shepherd (incidentally, the total opposite of Jesus the Good Shepherd. It makes one wonder how the cosmic Christ can be a sex-mad criminal one moment and the Son of God the next.) Hinduism is so diverse and has so many differences that you could meet six practising Hindus and think they belonged to totally different ways, or truths. One form of the religion has a Pantheon of gods, like the Greeks from whom it partly originated. Another form denies there is any god. Advaita Vedanta is the most common form of Hinduism; Jainism the most ancient, and then there are the Sikhs.

In the Islamic faith, Muhammad downgraded Jesus from the Son of God to a prophet. Muslims believe that Muhammad is the greatest prophet. The Sunni Muslims, the orthodox majority, follow the prophet's teachings. A separate branch of the Sunnis are the Wahabis in Saudi

Arabia. A large minority, the Shiite Muslims who control Iran, follow the teachings of Muhammad's brother-in-law, Ali. Salvation for Muslims is not by faith in Christ or a Christ figure, so much as in the fivefold duties: reciting the creed; praying five times a day; giving alms; fasting for Ramadan; and accomplishing the hajj (Mecca pilgrimage) at least once.

The New Ager who insists that the cosmic Christ appeared in the forms of Buddha, Krishna, Jesus, Muhammad and others, needs to examine his religious and academic integrity and fairness. A Muslim would be deeply offended by his proposals. The committed Buddhist and fervent Hindu would also have more than a few objections. The liberal wing of Christianity might be satisfied with such a Christ figure, but traditional orthodox Christians would certainly not be amused.

Liberal Christians and New Agers join together in wanting all men to experience closer ties in brotherly love and understanding. But if they try to achieve this end by insulting and distorting people's religions on a worldwide basis, they are going to cause the precise problem they are trying to avoid.

Those who mix up religions as though they are merely ingredients in a fruit-and-nut-cake, are being less than fair. They end up with a fruit-and-nut-case Christ, unable to make up his own befuddled consciousness from one generation, and one culture, to the next.

The view of Christ held by the New Age Christian tendency is so inadequate that it is understandable why they cannot accept him as the Saviour. They have to add salvation by faith in reincarnation...

11. Salvation by Faith in...
a Hundred Thousand Lifetimes

Thursday

Surprise has caught me out. I suddenly realise that my face is sagging and my mouth is hanging open. I gather it back into the neutral researcher look and ask Aussie Helen — still talking to me despite last night — if I have heard her correctly. Had I really understood her approach to the gassing of six million Jews?

'Sure,' drawls the Perth accent, unaffected by my reaction, 'it was their karma in the sense that they chose it or attracted it to themselves for some reason.'

'What about, say, a mad gunman who runs amok in a town?' I ask, trying to see how far Helen will go. 'What of his victims?'

She tells me that I have to realise that 'the people who get mown down by the guy shooting, in my opinion have already chosen to die...doesn't matter in what way they die. We see it as suffering. They don't. By the time we're dealing with it, they've gone to the other side. It's just another lesson in one more lifetime for them...It's part of the learning process...You have to realise that death is not the be-all and end-all, I mean, we have other lifetimes.'

But what of the people who cause these atrocities, the Adolf Hitlers of life? According to Helen and not a few others in the New Age movement, society makes its own Hitlers. Society produces its own reality. We get what we manufacture, no more, no less.

'Hitler was a symbol of the times,' explains Helen patiently, 'a symbol of the consciousness. He embodied the consciousness of that time.'

Modern woman Helen, with her Aussie confidence and outgoing vivacious ways, has life — or rather, her multilife existence — neatly packaged. Karma, the merciless law of consequences, unfolds without compassion or emotion in a never-ending string of reincarnations. What you sow in this life, you will reap in the next. We create our own personal reality. Society also creates its own reality — 'for we are all co-creators' — hence the starving Ethiopians.

This is one logical view of karma and reincarnation in the New Age. But it is only one of a rainbow of assessments. If Helen's is the ultraviolet view, then Dr Bloom would be infra-red.

'What I can't stand within the New Age movement,' he told me, 'and we frequently have open debates about this, are the you-create-your-own-reality people who say that humanity created Hitler as part of our reality, that it was a lesson we needed. The children who are starving in Somalia have created that reality for themselves as a lesson. I find that gung-ho, shallow expression of what is a seed of truth somewhere lacks any compassion and any wisdom, and I'm deeply hostile to it.'

Dr Bloom explained his own view of reincarnation, which he believed represented 'the major understanding of it in the New Age'.

'The soul is understood as a spark of God which doesn't fulfil its work of redemption in just one life. So it seeks in its own rhythm, like a seed that becomes a flower that produces another seed that becomes a flower, to do its work of redemption. As it travels the time that is between alpha and omega, it becomes more adept at creating a personality that's loving and christed, and it carries forward the lessons of its previous lives until, at some point, it has so understood the nature of sinfulness of this planet that it manages to produce a personality of unconditional love...The whole process is taking place within God's plan. Instead of 70 years, it is perhaps 700,000 years.'

I pointed out that I could not remember living before, so how could I remember the lessons of previous lives? Dr Bloom reassured me that he could take me to hundreds who have experienced past lives, as indeed has he.

'I once sat in meditation about fifteen years ago, and I thought myself a different persona,' shared Dr Bloom. 'I experienced myself as a young woman who had just taken her vows as a nun. In that experience, it highlighted for me certain aspects of my personality that were macho, aggressive, hard and bullying, and it brought in a female, feminine approach to deity that I desperately needed at the time.'

Dr Bloom detects the obvious question in my eyes, and the good doctor of psychology jumps in first.

'Now I give you that it may well have been my own subconscious throwing up a useful symbolic aspect of myself that was helpful.' Personally, he doesn't think so. 'In my own experience they [the previous lives] have a colour and a power and continually clothe themselves in historical dress, with certain memories of the time that they were in, and unavoidably I come to the conclusion that they are past-life memories.'

As a good psychologist, the doctor would also acknowledge that this final assessment could also be nothing more than aspects of his own psyche or a psychological quirk.

There are, of course, many other questions. If we all reincarnate, shouldn't there be a steady number of souls on planet Earth? Early known history speaks of maybe a couple of million on earth. Now there are nearly six thousand million. If we are all reincarnating, where have all the other millions come from?

What of the spirits channelled by New Agers? Some of these Red Indian chiefs claim to have been communicating for several lifetimes. Why haven't they reincarnated? Is the New Age in danger of wanting to have its cake and eat it by insisting that we all reincarnate except some souls that don't? And how many lifetimes will Hitler need in comparison to Mrs Bloggs, the village gossip? And will Mrs Bloggs have to wait for Adolf to catch up with her before she can enjoy whatever it is at the end of reincarnation, if anything? And who's organising karma and reincarnation? Is there some merciless computer keeping a tally of rights and wrongs, making sure the last drop of justice is squeezed out of each and every one of its victims?

And if so, what about the deity who is programming the computer? Hands up those who would want to go anywhere near him!!

Karma and reincarnation should also be questioned at the social level. These two pillars of doctrine are set in the foundations of philosophies which have held the East in poverty and degradation for centuries. Some Hindus will not even help desperate destitutes for fear of interfering with karma. The horrific fatalism stupefies action, and the matchstick legs and distended bellies of the starving millions are ignored. Mahatma Ghandi called reincarnation and karma 'a burden too great to bear'.

Does it not seem incredible that the West is now taking on board these deathly concepts? Opinion polls reveal that nearly twenty-five per cent of those under thirty in

Britain now believe in reincarnation. If I were God, I think I might weep a lot.

The Father of love stands there with his arms wide open, waiting for each of his prodigal offspring to run to him for his no-strings-attached forgiveness. But some of us, it seems, are determined to find our own way out of the pigsty, even if we have to wallow in it for a hundred thousand lifetimes (Lk 15:11 – 32).

God's answer to salvation sounds so simple. We trust him rather than ourselves.

We are on a loser if we bank on trusting ourselves. The Bible states that only one life has been ascribed to each human being (Heb 9:27; Rom 6:23), and we are all sinners who cannot save ourselves (Rom 3:10,23; Eph 2:8,9; Tit 3:5). Breaking just one tiny bit of the law means that we are guilty of breaking it all (Jas 2:10). That is the bad news. Now for the New Age good news: 'God loved the world so much that he gave us one hundred thousand lifetimes of hard labour and suffering until we learn to get it right.' Doesn't sound too good, this New Age good news, especially when compared to God's good news:

> For God so loved the world that he gave his one and only Son, that whoever believes in him shall not perish but have eternal life. For God did not send his Son into the world to condemn the world [and especially not to condemn it to a hundred thousand lifetimes], but to save the world through him (Jn 3:16,17).

It is God's love that is everlasting, not our suffering, and he loves us here and now, while we are in our sin, and without us having to scrub ourselves with the emery-paper of an earthly eternity (Jer 31:3; Is 13:11; Rom 5:8). We need to realise that we can share in Christ Jesus' righteousness; in Jesus we can be holy, totally redeemed and actually become the righteousness of God (Rom 6:10; Heb 7:27; 2 Cor 5:21).

His love was so great that he came in his one and only Son to pay the penalty for our sin, so that we could stand before him, holy and unblemished in his sight, and free from any accusation (Rom 5:8; Col 1:22). For our part, we have to turn from our ways — including reincarnation — and allow Jesus to save us for his own new age (Zech 1:3; 2 Pet 3:9; Rev 21:1ff). We have to accept him as Lord and to receive his Spirit within us (Jn 14:23; Jn 3:6; Rom 8:11).

Finally, we have to believe Jesus, and trust in him instead of ourselves (Jn 3:16; Eph 2:8,9; Rom 1:16). For New Age humanity, that is the hardest decision of all. The New Ager trusts only himself. There can be no suffering greater than for a father to live with the fact that his beloved children refuse to trust him.

Dr Bloom and the Christian New Age tendency especially need to reconsider one issue relating to salvation and reincarnation. The apostle Paul was at pains to hammer home that 'it is by grace you have been saved, through faith — and this not from yourselves, it is the gift of God — not by works, so that no one can boast' (Eph 2:8,9).

I am confident that Dr Bloom would be appalled at the idea of boasting before God. All I know is that if I had managed to attain perfect 'unconditional love', or whatever, after a hundred thousand lifetimes, I suspect that it would be almost impossible for me not to feel just a teensy-weensy bit of pride. Perhaps I might even turn to Jesus Christ and hint that I really did not need him to die for me after all. With a smug little smile, I might even point out that I had managed quite well on my own, thank you very much.

As you might expect by now, not all New Agers believe future salvation is through one of the above ways, but most would follow something similar, or a combination of one or more of them.

Many, of course, do not even talk in terms of salvation. Death for them is simply a return to some form of mass universal consciousness from which they may, or may not, return in another body, of one form or another, that might be animal, vegetable or mineral, at some future time, and that may be sooner or later or perhaps never.

For New Agers nothing is certain, except that they are certain that there is nothing that's certain.

12. A Wilting Angel, Slow Motion Kung-Fu, All Set to Music

Thursday lunch-time

'Tonight, it's Eileen.' I hear the excitement in one group member's whisper as she leaves the lunch-table.

It is not aimed in my direction, obviously. I get the distinct impression that the group think it would be a waste of time talking to me about Eileen Caddy. Understandable, I suppose. After all, how would I like it if at every other worship session during Spring Harvest or Keswick a New Ager kept posing awkward questions, jarring the spiritual atmosphere, and then delivering the final insult by declaring that only he was right? No matter how he did it, even with a smile and in a loving way, it would test one's patience to the limit.

Actually, when I think of the group's reaction to my 'narrow-minded, intolerable intolerance', they are behaving a good deal better than some of my Christian friends would in similar situations. These New Age rookies may have stopped flinging ecstatic arms around me, but they are still demonstrating a fair degree of civility and control. I can never accuse them of not trying to be beautiful people. Some, as I understood from discussions earlier in the week, even welcomed me as their 'thorn in the side', or even as a 'Christian conscience', as lapsed Catholic Christina put it. However, from the occasional odd look, I detect that three or four of them would now like to remove this particular thorn from their sides and put it firmly elsewhere!

Despite a hearty lunch of lettuce and other crunchy edibles, my angel (our 'inner life' lady, Amanda, had given each of us one on Sunday) is definitely wilting.

'Enthusiasm' turned out to be my angel, but I am still in Coventry, my teeth ache from the onslaught of over-crisp salads, and I have a lovely wife, two great children plus double egg and chips waiting at home.

The angels, Amanda had given us to understand, came from the etheric angelic levels. They were part of Findhorn's famous Transformation Game. 'The angels are the ones we have worked with and got to know,' she had explained. 'Having got to know them, we gave them suitable qualities as names.'

I have to confess that I have been treating my angel, Enthusiasm, with deep suspicion, especially since hearing that Findhorn also has its 'demon cards'.

'How are we supposed to conduct our inner life during the week?' a group member had asked.

'There came a time when Eileen Caddy's guide said one morning that there would be no more guidance to be shared,' replied Amanda. 'When Eileen asked why, she was told by her guide that those in the community were not to rely on gurus. Each was to have individual guidance.'

'How do we know if the guidance is coming from the right source?' I had asked.

'You'll know,' Amanda replied knowingly, 'or you'll get to know. Attune to whatever patch you're working on, then do what you feel should be done. It's like you're a tuning-fork. There is no official doctrine, no creed, we just seek inspiration where we individually resonate.'

This was where the 'angel cards' came in. Enthusiasm was in a family or angelic hierarchy of fifty-one others, including Humour, Patience, Harmony, Openness, Brotherhood, Strength, Freedom, Love, Integrity and so on. The demon cards were, of course, the opposites.

'If in doubt,' enthused Amanda, as though she'd borrowed my angel, 'ask for more information from your angel.'

To the Christian used to chatting things over with God, angel-talk is no big deal. If anything, it is a backward step. This, of course, is making the big assumption that they are angels and not the opposition in their Sunday best!

Thursday afternoon

The lady of the house squares up to me in the orchard, a female Bruce Lee, seemingly ready to spring into martial art action. Nona's 'thing' is tai chi ch'uan.

We're spending the afternoon at an associated Findhorn outpost, Newbold House. The tour over, Nona stands before me among the apple trees, and it is like watching a slow-motion replay of a kung-fu movie. The literal meaning of Nona's art is 'supreme ultimate fist', yet it has little to do with fighting. This is purely spiritual, a graceful, ballet-like series of stylised movements which can take up to a year to perfect. The exponent uses it to harmonise the flow through the body of what is called the universal energy, ch'i, or prana.

Martial arts are normally associated with China and South East Asia, but they probably originated from Indian monks who developed various forms of unarmed combat. It was wise to have something in the dangerous wild East, especially when your beliefs forbade you to carry weapons.

Just before our own King Harold got an eyeful of arrow around 1066, martial arts started spreading rapidly from the monastic communities. China took the early ideas and developed kung fu and tai chi ch'uan. India's home-grown version became Vadha or Vajra Vashta. Then the 'Do' (way of life, or spiritual discipline) began to be attached to them. This was especially true in Japan, with judo, kendo and laido, aikido, and the associated karate, ju-jitsu, kyudo and ninjutsu (television's Ninja turtle fans, take note). Korea, Thailand (kick-boxing), Vietnam and Okinawa have other lesser known martial arts.

Western armed forces brought judo to us just after the turn of this century, and a couple of World Wars and a shrinking globe brought us ju-jitsu, followed quickly by karate and aikido. Thanks to the Hong Kong movie industry, martial arts now make big business in the West and if children's television, comics and books have the same influence, these arts are here to stay and increase for the next generation or two.

All martial arts have a spiritual emphasis, unlike our own self-defence sports. The oriental arts have developed from a background of spiritual discipline and are still practised as part of Zen Buddhism, Taoism and the New Age. Some of the martial arts aspects are similar to some rituals and practices in modern-day British occultism. Many in the New Age, like our hostess Nona, use the spiritual form of the arts to plug into the cosmic force.

In local judo and karate clubs, you take your pick and take your chance. Many teach the way of the warrior and stress fighting technique. But the committed martial arts exponent will rarely miss out the oriental aspects of life style and spirituality.

And here lies the danger. Nona was a quiet, charming

lady who was physically in good shape thanks to tai chi ch'uan. Spiritually, it was a different story. She was hooked on Eastern spirituality, thanks to martial arts.

How does the Christian respond to his local club? The Christian Response to the Occult (CRO), in a helpful leaflet, gives three factors which need to be considered:

1 The teacher's intention to pass on the spiritual content of his art
2 The student's interest in martial arts as a form of spirituality
3 The traditional emphasis of any given style of martial arts upon 'Do' (life style and beliefs).[1]

Local yoga club members may do well to ask themselves the same questions. It may be that they simply want to keep fit or lessen the stress of high-powered living, but they may get more than they bargained for.

As a personal choice, I would prefer one of dozens of home-grown sports, keep-fit schemes and stress reducing hobbies, none of which has hidden spiritual dangers.

Perhaps this is an area into which the local church might consider moving, as was suggested towards the end of Chapter 8. Stress beating keep fit groups based on thoroughly biblical principles might well prove an evangelistic opportunity as well as a positive contribution to community life.

Should the church be giving the Nonas of this world an alternative? Careful with this question: God might expect you to do something about it if you answer yes.

Even in Nona's orchard we could hear music. Everything seems to be done to New Age music, whether it be stylised, slow-moving martial arts, deep-seated meditation, preparing the teatime celery soup or cleaning out the toilets. It haunts the atmosphere and sets up a strange contradiction.

The New Age is supremely romantic in its rose-tinted outlook on the world and humanity. There is love and warmth as people hug and attune to each other's intimate inner beings. And yet much of the music contradicts all this with a cold, pristine, brittle quality. You could imagine it being recorded in a hospital theatre by well scrubbed artistes playing clinically disinfected instruments.

Ultra-clean, ethereal, synthesised sound vibrates the mind, accompanied by the mating calls of lovelorn whales and the lonely squeaks of the dolphin. The backing choruses are made up of chanting monks, Chinese gongs and the ubiquitous didgeridoos. The surge of sound is often reminiscent of an ice-cold Antarctic cascade, or the wailing winds trapped in telephone wires. In fact, one New Age company produces nothing but wind sounds — 'the songs of the universe' — which are caught by the strings of elevated eolian harps and greatly amplified.

New Age music claims to affect the mind and consequently to be a new listening experience. On this score, it is actually older than Johann Sebastian Bach.

Bach was commissioned to write a lively but calming number to relax an insomniac Russian envoy. Writing in the highly structured and mathematically precise baroque style, Bach successfully produced a steady, slow-moving largo, and the envoy fell fast asleep.[2] Other baroque movements, played at a particular rhythm of around sixty beats per minute, were produced by Handel, Vivaldi and Telemann. It was left until the 1970s for scientists to explain that certain music could slow down the body processes and induce a meditative state.[3]

Supremely, New Agers are atmosphere engineers, and music is just one way of seducing the senses. It is often combined with colour or herbal aromatherapy and warmth so that two or more senses are beguiled and ravished. New Age music seeks to lull; to seep beneath, around and inside the mind; to draw the listener down into the subterranean unknown of the unconscious. This is a form of mind-manipulation, much used in most fields of British occultism like witchcraft and satanism, and is a way of altering the state of consciousness. The vast majority of New Agers, of course, are oblivious to this link.

The discerning Christian is called to remain sober, alert and ever mindful of deceptions (1 Pet 1:13; 4:7; 5:8; Tit 2:12; 1 Thess 5:6). Certainly, the Christian can use music to lift, inspire and enjoy, for in many ways music can certainly seem like the food of love. But too much for the wrong reasons can be poisonous and can be just as potent as overindulging in other ways. The promotional leaflet accompanying New World Cassettes explains New Age sound as:

> Music that explores beyond the edge of your consciousness and reveals the 'Death Experience' for what it is; a journeying of arriving…Plaintive flutes and superb sound effects tenderly enfold your consciousness to elevate and reassure you repeatedly. This is music of immensity, or rare beauty and sensitivity, a music that speaks to and reassures our very soul, reminding us of the delight, the deep joy and preciousness of the complete cycle of life.

Christian music critic Clive Manning wrote in his assessment of New Age music,

> Alice Bailey…regarded as a key figure in the Theosophical Society, which brought New Age into being, laid great importance on music. She taught that music was to be part of the preparation for the New Age. The idea of opening yourself up to New Age music rings many alarm-bells. It underlines the fact

that we must always remain the master and never become the slave of any art form.[4]

The beautiful Lorelei and Sirens of legend beguiled and shipwrecked sailors with their irresistible music. Myths often have their origin in fact. The truth in this case is that man can be lured beyond sense and endurance and music is one way of doing it.

13. A Lady Called Eileen

Thursday evening

The resemblance is uncanny. She looks just like Mary Whitehouse, complete with silver-white hair, smile and looks. The style of glasses and the neat, well-made flowered suit make them almost twins. The accent is different, though the definite and distinct ways of speaking are the same. Even the words Eileen Caddy uses might have come from the mouth of the nation's moral grandmother…some of them, at least.

'Let the words of God manifest in us…a change of life is the first step towards wholeness…we need to really forgive…I use prayer a lot…God has been there helping me every step of the way…bring love into everything …next time you come up against an enemy, try loving…'

I cannot help but warm to Eileen Caddy. It is not so much that I have been a fan of Mary Whitehouse since she started the National Viewers' and Listeners' Association in the permissive past; it is more to do with Eileen Caddy herself. She sits in the midst of our group, radiating her own charm and warmth; a seventy-two-year-old grandma with a compelling personality who is to keep the group spellbound.

As I warm to her, I listen and then the sadness comes. There is much to agree with, but just as much to query.

Questioning Eileen is as daunting as I imagine it could be for a researcher facing her 'twin'. Both know who they are, what they are, what they believe and why they believe. Both are unshakable. Mary Whitehouse would sit on the foundation of Jesus Christ and God's written word. Eileen Caddy sits just as firmly on the 'rock of her inner guidance', which she claims is God's word for her and others today.

The problem is that there is a contradiction between God's word in the Bible and Eileen's 'inner voice'.

Rather than quote Eileen's spoken word, we turn to her written biography, *Flight to Freedom*, in which she says, 'To learn to turn within for God's guidance has become the purpose of my life.'[1]

But God tells his people to turn for guidance to his word and Law, which 'is God-breathed and is useful for teaching, rebuking, correcting and training in righteousness' (2 Tim 3:16; Josh 1:8; Deut 29:29). The Bible, however, did not play much part in the Caddy family, though Eileen herself uses parts of it on occasions.[2] Inside is the last place to go, according to classical teaching on Christian guidance. We can fool ourselves too easily, and our inner promptings should only be considered in the full light of God's word, the circumstances he has put us in and the advice of others who are in touch with the Lord.

Eileen's story continues; this time she is quoting husband Peter:

> We meditated together, and Naomi [a friend] channelled a message from a great spiritual being who told her that she and I had been together in many lifetimes…[3]

God's word is against those who act as mediums, as we have already noted, and he offers only one life followed by resurrection rather than an endless trial of earthly existences (Lev 19:31; 20:6; 1 Sam 28:7–20; 1 Chron 10:13; Heb 9:27; 1 Cor 15).

The next problem with Eileen's beliefs is of a personal nature, and so I hand over to her to tell of it in her own words. It concerns the decision of Peter to leave his first wife, Sheena, and for Eileen to divorce husband Andrew and leave her five young children:

> The voice went on: 'You have taken a very big step...But if you follow my voice all will be well. I have brought you and Peter together for a very special purpose...Be still and know that I am God.'
>
> Peter and Sheena were convinced that I had heard God's own voice. I wasn't at all sure, and yet if I accepted what I heard, it must be the voice of God. The more I thought about it, the more concerned I became. I remember the people God spoke to in the Bible. But those were special people with God's special tasks to do. Why should He speak to a woman who had left her husband and children to 'live in sin' with another man?
>
> And yet here was this very clear voice telling me to listen and all would be well in my life. My thoughts kept turning to the Ten Commandments. The word 'adultery' plagued me. The voice said I was doing the right thing...[4]

To be fair, Eileen herself had the same suspicions that some may now be having about the origin of her voices. At this time, Eileen was being dominated by Sheena, who was still officially married to Peter.

She [Sheena] was firmly convinced that God is within each of us, and that we are an expression of God. Her 'training' was to reinforce our faith in this inner God and to encourage us to follow it in our lives.

In my case Sheena was faced with terrific resistance. I had not come to her of my own free will, nor was I searching consciously for the meaning of God in my life. I wasn't even sure it was God's voice I continued to hear. Least of all did I believe that the vivid visions I was beginning to have were divinely inspired.

For all I knew they may have been the work of the devil or caused by some emotional distress. The only reason I was there was Peter.[5]

Sheena dominated her husband's mistress and assured her that there would come a time when 'there won't be the slightest shadow of a doubt which voice is the voice of God, and you will follow no other'.[6] Eileen wrote, 'So I gave Sheena complete power over me.'[7] At this time, Eileen said she had to suffer the shame of having two babies 'out of wedlock'. Also around this time she received a court order to stay away from the children of her first marriage until they were eighteen. Her first husband thought Eileen 'was bewitched by Peter and Sheena'.[8] Following the birth of a third child (by which time Peter and Eileen were married), the 'inner voice' had a special word:

My beloved child, it was I who joined you and Peter together to be made a perfect whole for My glory. I have much for you and Peter to do and because of this work I do not require you to have any more babies.

Eileen was subsequently sterilised.[9]

Peter, Eileen and the three children moved into hotel management and though this was successful at the beginning it came to an end when they were dismissed for an unknown reason. They, together with a friend, Dorothy Maclean, moved to a caravan park near Findhorn. It was here that they were to become 'a beacon of light...and God's fortress', attracting 'the young and old, all nations, all colours, all creeds... in perfect peace and harmony...'[10]

They conversed with the devas, the spirits of nature, as they grew their plants. They played classical music and recorded bird songs because this was what the plants enjoyed and preferred.[11] And by eating the right plants in the right frame of mind, accepting that they were nurtured by spirits, the trio and the children would build themselves up with the life-force.[12] (An appropriate description of panentheism — God or the life-force in everything.)

The conflict between Eileen's inner voice and God's word continues:

> I began to study the lectures on Positive Thinking...I felt very silly sitting by myself repeating 'I am power, I am truth, I am love'...Gradually my attitude began to change...I had made a breakthrough...In the stillness I received: 'This is the most important thing you have ever learned in your life, and because of it your life has changed. You have been born again into the new, and the old is no more.'[13]

God's word states that it is God's Holy Spirit that brings new life, not positive thinking (Jn 3:1–21).

Eileen turned to Christ with an invitation to come into her life. But it was the wrong Christ.

> I realised that if I can accept that God is within me,
> why can I not accept the Christ within?…I knew
> without a shadow of doubt that I am a beautiful
> Christ-filled being…To be a Christed being, to fully
> claim my Christhood, means to transmute the negative
> into the positive every moment of every day…Some
> call it the Christ, others call it something else. The
> most important thing is that as more and more people
> recognise the power of this inner energy, the more
> we will lift the vibrations of the planet together.[14]

In Chapter 10, we dealt with the sadness of those who
place their trust in salvation by faith in a false Christ
figure. Reading Eileen's autobiography, the word 'sadness'
seems appropriate. It is the story of a woman struggling
with many personal inadequacies, all of which she
honestly details. There is the bleakness of missing her first
five children, the near-suicidal depressions, the
despondency of being a pawn, first of Sheena, then of
Peter and always of the inner voice. There is the dejection
of low self-esteem, the agonies of jealousy when her
second husband sees other women, and throughout all
this, the only anchor she has is a God who is continually
telling her to brace herself and think positive thoughts.

The horror and sadness of New Age thinking is at last
laid bare when Eileen comes to the logical conclusion of
her search. She has to recognise that there is only herself
on which to rely. For she is the Christ. She is God — the
ultimate in positive thinking.

In a letter to Peter, who by this time has divorced
Eileen for somebody else, she writes:

> But now something has happened to me and I realise
> that I AM the guidance. At long last I know that God
> and I are one, that I am a co-creator with God…I am
> a Christed being. I found this difficult to accept to

begin with, but as I affirmed this daily, I began to realise that I AM it.[15]

On her way to the realisation of her Godhood, Eileen came to recognise that she was also part of a growing New Age concept — the soul ray. This is the principle that there are archetypal figures in the universe and many souls can be elevated on to the rays that belong to these figures. For Eileen, it was the Mary ray.

> I was told, 'You are Mary, the mother of Jesus the Christ.' When I questioned that, God had asked me if I could accept it as a Ray of which many people were an expression. That made perfect sense to me, as I had felt an affinity with Mary from childhood.[16]

And,

> I was intrigued by the connection between Quan Yin and Mary…Soon after that, in meditation, I saw myself entering a shrine or chapel. It was quite dark inside. At the other side of the room I saw the figure of Quan Yin. As I came closer, she said: 'I have been waiting for you.' Then Quan Yin blessed me…I feel the presence of Quan Yin and Mary overlighting me…In my travels all over the world they have appeared to me in visions, as well as in a more concrete form.[17]

Eileen picked up the hint in meditation that she was to be instrumental in bringing the East of Quan Yin and the West of Mary together, and was subsequently delighted to receive an invitation to lead workshops and speak at an international peace conference in India.

What concerned me was the description of just who Quan Yin is. The comments in brackets are mine:

> Quan Yin is the ancient Chinese symbol of the World
> Mother [similar to the Western pagan Mother Earth
> goddess], and is representative of the feminine
> principle of creation; the Mother aspect of deity. The
> feminine principle has been represented throughout
> history by many names...Mother Kundalini [source of
> the serpent force said to be coiled around the base of
> the human spine], Isis [Egyptian goddess much called
> upon in modern occultism], Sophia [see below], the
> Virgin Mary. The unfolding new age foretold by the
> prophets has as its keynote the conscious restoration
> of the Golden Balance between the masculine and
> feminine principles. This Golden Balance is to be
> found in the hearts of all people; and is none other
> than the True Self. Know the balance by honouring its
> source which is the True Self. Love is your very
> nature. God dwells with you, as YOU.[18]

The story of Sophia mentioned above seems very apt for
Eileen Caddy. Sophia was the gnostic aeon of wisdom
who was seduced by a demon. She thought a ray of light
was coming from the Father but its source was in fact a
demon. Sophia followed the ray and fell into the abyss of
Chaos.

Our elegant hostess has kept the group enthralled. From
my seat in Coventry I risk one or two questions.

ME: You speak as one with authority...

EILEEN: (laughing)...Or experience.

ME: Most people have spoken to us this week in tentative
ways. They have offered us things to try. You tell us what
to do. Why is there this difference? Why your authority?

EILEEN: It works for me. It doesn't necessarily mean it will
work for you. Try it. If it works for you, lovely. Use it.

ME: On the question of God, you talk of praying to your
higher self, and yet you say your higher self is God?

EILEEN: God is in each of us. God is in everything.

ME: (testing how firmly her mind is closed on this idea) Is there in your understanding a God who is outside of his creation as well as inside?

EILEEN: God is in everything. So God is in nature; God is in each of us. That's the realisation we have come to. (She leans towards me.) Can you accept the God in you?

ME: I can accept that I'm made in God's image.

EILEEN: (becoming quite evangelistic and not wishing to let this young upstart off the hook) Yes, but can you not say, 'I am God'?

ME: I have invited Jesus Christ into my life as my Lord and Saviour.

EILEEN: God is in you!

ME: I agree, but I see God also as the separate Creator.

EILEEN: (the evangelist's finger is now raised for emphasis) And you are a co-creator with God — *right*! Are you not a co-creator with God?

ME: No. I can work with what God gives me, but I cannot create. That's the Lord's job.

Focaliser Terry is getting nervous of the questioning and moves the discussion on to other subjects. Eileen and I agree to differ. As hostess, it is her floor and she takes it for the last word. She speaks of receiving her inner voice for thirty-seven years, a voice with which she has fallen in love. It tells her, 'There is no separation.'

The evening ends with her smiling serenely, with the style of the Queen Mum. I can almost picture her in the dream of which she writes at the end of her book. She wonders about its meaning…

> In the dream Peter and I were brought together…we were to be crowned king and queen…We were in a huge, beautiful garden. The trees were old and yet

> they looked as if they had just been planted...It was
> all so new and yet so old...We were dressed for our
> coronation...We had very important work to do and
> we had to do it together...[19]

The Queen Mum looks at us as the group comes to the
conclusion of her evening audience.

'This is where I have reached in my evolution. What
the next stage is I do not know. This is my experience. I
just share it with you.'

It summed up the audience, yet it is also the essence
of the whole New Age movement — bright people
striving to be beautiful with only an unknown inner voice
or unguided experience to light their paths.

I walk out quietly, thanking an amazingly gracious and
loving God who has not left us in the dark but has
provided his word as 'a lamp to my feet and a light for my
path'.

I look back on a twenty-year journey along that lighted
path with gratitude and inwardly weep for Eileen, for
focalisers Terry and Marjorie, for the questioning Jenny
and Tom, for Aussie Helen, and Renata who poshly
enunciates the Kaiser's German, and all the rest of the
group whom I shall never meet again after tomorrow. I
wonder what more I might have done to witness to an
Almighty Power who has the face of love, the Number
One Personality who stands above, and yet is within his
measureless universe. I place them all into his hands.

Maybe I'll send them a copy of the book when it's
finished.

14. How to Help 1
— *Chaos of Morals*

During the last few years of ministry and research, some principles have been tried and found useful. They have been tested at Findhorn, Glastonbury's famous Festival of Contemporary Performing Arts, pagan New Age festivals, Earthweek events, psychic New Age fairs, Monkton Wylde New Age centre, The Wrekin Trust, St James', Piccadilly, Festivals of Mind, Body and Spirit, and in discussions with leaders and many members of the New Age movement. The principles are not infallible nor comprehensive, and you will no doubt be able to extend them and fill them out with your own thoughts.

Before highlighting special approaches to New Agers, first a brief résumé of what should be the normal Christian response, no matter whom we are helping:

1   **Listen and love.** There is nothing so off-putting to any person, be he New Ager or old codger, than to be attacked by a Bible-thumping zealot whose only concern is to discharge his religious duty of spouting the good news. We need to spend time with people, loving and caring and earning the right to be invited into their private spiritual lives.

2   Enlist help — God's first! Only a fool talks to others on spiritual matters without first conversing with God. The New Age rebel glories in being God, and no amount of verbiage on its own will change that. Only prayer and the consequent action of the real God can bring surrender. It is at once the evangelist's greatest frustration that he cannot of himself win people over, but also the greatest faith builder to see the Holy Spirit do it in his own good time.

Second, enlist at least one other Christian as you reach out; the spiritual soloists often end up playing on their own without adequate help and prayer support. Jesus made it clear that Christianity was teamwork. Half the Christian churches in my area and elsewhere supported me during my research, which was often undertaken in partnership with my wife, Linda, or others. I made sure of a double portion of prayer support when I was forced to go solo at Findhorn. Remember the biblical norm: Jesus sent his followers out in pairs (Lk 10:1ff).

3   Be prepared. Understand the people to whom you go. Not only study the New Age through books like this, but keep abreast of developments on the New Age in the religious press. This is an ever-changing, multi-faceted movement, not a static display. No matter how prepared we might be, we will get out of our depth at times and we need the humility to call in others more experienced.

This is especially true for those who are, or become, mentally or emotionally disturbed. Some Christians have the quaint and harmful notion that psychiatry is obsolete in the face of Christian prayer and healing. When the mind snaps, a psychiatrist — Christian or not — is essential, just as much as the casualty doctor is when a leg breaks. In many cases, I insist that a disturbed person visits a GP for a check-up as a condition of my continued help.

4 **Do focus on the main points**. Love people rather than pet theories or hobby-horses. Valuable time can be lost denouncing alternative life styles, Gaia, New Age leaders or whatever. There is such a thing as Christian positive thinking which concentrates, not on negative criticism, but on the abundance of a positive relationship with Jesus Christ. We will eventually have to introduce a note of caution and criticism among New Agers, but the emphasis should always be on an introduction to the Lord who alone can put things right.

Now to the specifics of helping New Agers.

Allow New Agers to see their moral chaos

But be gentle. It can be quite devastating for a sensitive, seeking New Ager to discover that his path ahead is laid across quicksand, and that his destination is merely a mirage. The hope shimmering in the future has kept him going and now you are going to tell him that it is non-existent. It is doomed to evaporate when the heat of life gets too much, for there is no substance, no fixtures, no absolutes — in fact, none of the recognised pillars that hold society together. It is all hot air.

A Channel 4 producer telephoned me as I was thinking out this point to ask for help with a programme on ritual child abuse. As we chatted, it dawned on me that the lady was a typical London New Age guppie (green and upwardly mobile), and I shuddered to realise that she was not as much bothered about child abuse as about producing a juicy slot for the box. In a rather self-righteous way, she shared her revulsion over the subject, and I decided to test the lady's world.

'Why does it repulse you so much?' I challenged, forgetting my own advice on being gentle.

'I'm sorry. What did you say?' The distant voice obviously thought she had misheard.

'I wondered why you thought the practice of ritual child abuse was so wrong.'

'Of course it's wrong,' she snorted. 'Everybody knows it's wrong!'

'Yes, but why?'

'Because it goes against everything we accept is right.'

'But who are we to judge what is right or wrong?' I persisted. 'Everybody today reckons we should do what is right in our own eyes.'

'Right,' the producer agreed firmly. 'And if everybody did that, society would be a much better place.'

'Are you sure?' I queried. 'Let's say you want to go sailing this weekend but a satanist wants to abuse children. You both think what you are doing is right. What right have you to say that sailing is fine and abuse is wrong? What gives you the right to criticise the satanist's choice if it is all right to do what is right in our own eyes?'

There was a pause in the conversation.

We went on to speak of the rise in the occult and satanism in a world which had killed off God and his Ten Commandments and replaced them with six billion mini-gods, each wanting to do what was right in their own eyes. The lady producer thought I was a bit old-fashioned and would not fit into her view of how her programme should run. Our conversation sadly ended.

When we throw away the rule book and the referee, such things as right and wrong and truth also depart.

I remember six of us playing Monopoly once. The boot and the iron wanted to buy property the first time round, but the rest said no. That could only be done on the second circuit. Then the car and the top-hat joined forces and played together, while the others called them cheats.

The ship decided to buy hotels without first getting the required number of houses.

'Are you sure you can't find the rule book?' the cry went up, not for the first time.

The game — played, incidentally, between upright theological students training for the Christian ministry — eventually exploded into anarchy when the dog refused to go to jail.

There is only one alternative left when the rule book is lost: you play from memory. When that begins to fade, then all have equal rights to make up the laws. More likely, it provides an opportunity for the more strong-headed or noisy majority to get their way. Right and wrong have little to do with it, because these categories have been replaced by personal whim.

The society which accepts that all is relative and that people must do what is right in their own eyes and according to their own situation, must logically accept that the satanist can abuse children if he thinks it is right for him to do so.

If, on the other hand, society wants to insist that some things are absolutely wrong, then it must have a firm moral basis on which to stand. It is not sufficient simply for one part of society, even the majority, to make that stand. It is too easy for life's 'dogs' to refuse to play the game.

The establishment in the West and its authority have been under attack for several generations now, but it is still getting away with setting standards because the majority of people are still 'playing from memory'. There is still a large residue of our Christian heritage which obeyed an external absolute referee — God — and his book of ten rules. How long this will last in a society which increasingly knows God and Jesus only as swear words, and laughs uproariously at the antiquated Bible and its Ten Commandments, is anybody's guess.

15. How to Help 2
— Questions to Ask.
Applying the Gospel

New Agers tell us that man is about to take a quantum leap in his evolution and rise to a higher level of consciousness. The world will consequently undergo a beneficial change, ushering in a new, caring, sharing era. Through reincarnation, we will continue to improve until we realise our essential divinity. Faced with this, it seems reasonable for Christians to make the first move...

Approach with questions

These New Age beliefs beg endless questions. Christians should feel at liberty to ask them, and to require that any answers should make reasonable sense. The Christian can afford to probe and question quietly, realising that at the end of each New Age argument there is a void which requires a massive leap of blind faith.

1 How do they know mankind is going to improve when it has never happened before in world history (ignoring the guess-work of evolution) and there is no evidence for it happening today? Do they not suspect that they may be losing touch with reality?

2   Do they think that they might have manufactured this belief because otherwise the future looks so bleak for mankind?

3   Could . it be that the New Age has been cobbled together by people who hate the idea of having to worship anybody but themselves? And in this case, doesn't the story of man's rebellion against God begin to make good sense?

4   Are New Agers perhaps being conned by the expectations that build up at the approach of every new epoch? History teaches us that there were massive expectations in society at the beginning of the second millennium, and that since there have been notable (and unreal) expectations of change for every new century and even at the beginning of a new decade.

5   Is it wise for people to allow their lives to be guided by lumps of matter whizzing through space?

6   Is it not a worry when a person's love life depends on a blob of wet tea-leaves at the bottom of a cup?

(It is sometimes helpful to know the shortcomings of astrology, or positive thinking, or whatever, and to challenge New Agers in these areas, but we need always to keep the focus on Jesus and the good news.)

7   What is to happen to men and women who have nothing to worship? Every society there has ever been has had gods. Now we are told that we are God. Are we to worship ourselves? If so, are we worth it? And if we think so now, will we think so when an accident puts us flat on our backs, only to discover that there is nobody to look up to?

8   Who made Gaia? Whether or not planet Earth is a living organism, possessing powers to rejuvenate itself, is not an issue we need to dwell on for too long. There are more important questions. Who or what caused the earth to exist? Who or what designed it? What was before Gaia

or earth? What massive intellect lies behind the combined impressive intellect of mankind? Which incredible designer is responsible for the snowflake and the intricacies of the human body? Is it intelligent simply to say intelligence came from a primordial blob of mud in a stagnant pond, or from a big bang in space? And anyway, what could cause a big bang and who was responsible for the basic laws of physics and mathematics that had to be present for such an explosion to take place?

9 What do New Agers think about the Christian story?

Caution is needed with this question. It is amazing what some New Agers have come to believe about our faith and especially about Jesus. Learn how to give a one-minute rundown from start to finish, involving a loving Creator, a rebellious devil and mankind who told God to go where they themselves deserved to be; the consequent sin of separation and selfishness; the never-say-die, unbreakable, elastic love of a Father who refused to take mankind's 'no' as a final answer and a Saviour who came to redeem the lost; the Holy Spirit's power to create a new man; and a King of kings who has a new age planned that will put present human ideas to shame. The good news, shared sensitively and with prayer, can warm the most hardened New Ager, even those who thought Christianity had passed its sell-by date.

Remember as you challenge that you are not out to score points. Whenever you win an argument in evangelism you are in danger of losing a soul. The questions are simply exercises in encouraging New Age friends to face the reality before their very eyes, rather than continue seeking some illusory, make-believe reality within themselves. Let us gently insist that they look honestly into the enormous voids at the ends of their arguments.

Be prepared to answer questions

You can be sure that many New Agers will be able to give some good answers to the above questions. Some, in fact, will do it with a zeal and love that can put Christians to shame.

Each of us is called to be a witness, to stand up and tell others of what Jesus has done for us (Acts 1:8). But the good witness needs to face cross-examination.

The phenomenal rise in paganism and the occult and in New Age philosophies is partly attributable to the church's appalling and lazy witness in the last two generations. Sometimes, we have just not bothered. At other times, our witness has been weak or contradictory. Imagine this scenario...

'Yer honour,' stammers the witness for the prosecution in a road accident case, 'I saw this man — at least, it looked like a man — walk out into the middle of the road — on second thoughts, maybe he was on the pavement. Anyway, the important thing is that he shouted out that he was going to throw himself under the next lorry that passed, though I didn't actually hear him...er...that's what my mate who was with me at the time said that he had said, yer honour...er...though to be honest, my mate wouldn't swear on the Bible that that was precisely what the man shouted. Now, where was I? Oh, yes, this man, or whoever, jumped or was pushed or fell under...'

Not a very convincing witness. The judge would have dismissed his testimony and rightly directed the jury to ignore it. Now consider this...

'Yer honour,' stammer some modern Christian witnesses, 'there was this man — or God-man, or maybe he just looked as if he was filled with God. Anyway, he said a lot of good things, though it's hard to know exactly what he did say because we can't trust hand-me-down stories and history…However, setting that aside, we can say we think that he existed and cured the blind and fed thousands with a handful of butties…though, to be fair, many say these were just stories made up to get over the truth that he was a remarkable man…No, no, they weren't lies, so much as what they call myths. You see, in those days they were ignorant men, not educated like what we are, and so they invented these stories — like Jesus being raised from the dead and being born of a virgin — so that we would see what a clever man he was…Yes, I realise that he wasn't that clever if he didn't actually rise from the dead, but that's not the point, is it? The main point is that I am standing up to be a witness to him…No, I've not met him, but I've read a lot about him in my theological books…'

Much of the Christian witness of the past generations has been similar to this, and sometimes much worse. Today's Christian advocate needs to know his apologetics instead of constantly apologising for not knowing them. Christian bookshops are full of books on how we know there is a personal God, why we can rely on the Bible as God's written word, how we can be sure that the Jesus of the Gospels is the real historical Jesus. As witnesses, we desperately need to get back to the Bible and actually read it and ask the Holy Spirit, who wrote it in men's minds, to reveal the truth to us. Perhaps we should not spend all our valuable quiet-time relying solely on daily Bible-reading notes. Great though they are, they can get between us and God and his word sometimes.

Be a good witness. Learn to know what to say when cross-examined.

Spiritual health warning

Such appeals as above used to leave me in the pits of despair, especially as a raw recruit to Christianity. I really did try my best to be a good witness but it was mostly gibberish that poured out. I often felt like a deflated second-rate citizen and my only consolation was the apostle Paul, who spoke 'in weakness and fear, and with much trembling' (1 Cor 2:3). Looking back, I am amazing how God used my weakness to reveal his strength (2 Cor 12:10). Today, I am saddened that sometimes my own strength is my greatest weakness. God can use those who rely on him more than those who rely on themselves. But having noted this, the Lord would still have us build up our knowledge as his witnesses. Just try to avoid thinking you're God's answer to the New Age, or whatever.

Applying the gospel

The starting point in presenting the good news to New Agers is important. Begin with the common ground:

We both agree that we are killing ourselves with poisons and pesticides. We accept joint stewardship of ourselves and our planet. Our doctrines of wholeness and health are similar. We hold hands in the fight against materialism and the idolatry of modern science. We exalt the spiritual side of man and together reach for the mystical. We both speak of love, togetherness, harmony, restoration and peace.

As we spend time on reaffirming common beliefs, it helps to establish relationships (New Agers need to relate to you before Jesus), it corrects any false notions of Christianity (there are many in the New Age) and it builds up trust.

Speak of sin too early and you may as well talk double-Dutch! Sin to New Agers is human ignorance or a break in harmony between people or things. Take them to Calvary too soon and they will wonder what all the fuss is about. Why should anyone have to be sacrificed on a cross for something that is nobody's fault? Surely, nobody is to blame for ignorance. In any case, when everybody is doing what is right in their own eyes, nobody can say who is right and wrong. We need to work our way towards the God of holiness who gave up his Ten Commandments.

If the Christian evangelist starts his conversation with truth or God, a kaleidoscope of totally inappropriate images will surface for New Agers, who have been nurtured on the *Star Trek* diet. For a generation, you could say that this cult television programme has almost been the star ship of the New Age line, though to be fair, the programme has also promoted many Christian values concerning good and evil. However, many of those aboard the latest *Enterprise* are technicolor New Agers in science-fiction dress, mixing reality with large portions of fantasy. Here are the men and women that we can evolve into, some with highly developed psychic powers. Reality can be what we make it. The world of thought is what is real and powerful.

Take the following scene, for example…

Star Date:	Unknown.
Position:	Millions of light-years away from their normal galaxy beat.
Problem:	Can the time traveller who took them there get them back?
CAPTAIN:	What got us here?
TRAVELLER:	Thought.
CAPTAIN:	Thought?
TRAVELLER:	Thought. You do understand, don't you, that thought is the basis of all reality? The energy of thought…is very powerful.
CREW MEMBER:	That's not an explanation.

TRAVELLER:	I have the ability to act like a lens which focuses thought.
CREW MEMBER:	(*laughing*) That's just, er...so much nonsense. You're asking us to believe in magic!
TRAVELLER:	(*smiling*) Well, yes. This could seem like magic to you.
CAPTAIN:	No. No. This actually makes sense to me. Only the power of thought could explain what has been happening.
TRAVELLER:	Thought is the essence of where you are now. You do understand the danger, don't you?
CAPTAIN:	Chaos! What we think is what happens!

Here in a nutshell conversation is a big part of the New Age. Such thinking is also similar to the bedrock concepts of paganism and the occult.

Before talking with New Agers about reality and truth, we need to spend time on the whole subject of spirituality, and also the identity of the forces which they contact when they voyage through inner space. They are often going in dangerous crafts where no man has safely gone before. We need to dwell on the dangers of the good and the bad in the spiritual realms and challenge their gullibility. They need to understand that there is good and bad in everything, including the spiritual world. They should not be too surprised if they plunge recklessly into spirituality and meet a power which they don't know, they don't understand and which eventually they cannot control. There are no neutral powers in the spiritual world.

So, we need to progress from the common ground to the spiritual, and perhaps then to the lack of control man seems to show in these areas. Then we can talk about sin;

then we might get a hearing for the Saviour of mankind; then we can come to the cross of Calvary; then the New Ager might be willing to consider the real new age promised by God.

One leaflet which does this superbly is *I Want to Be Who I Am. I Want to Be Whole* from the Christian Publicity Organisation (see end of Chapter 17).

16. How to Help 3
— God's New Age.
Credit to the New Age

New Agers have sung about the dawning of the Age of Aquarius since the sixties. Some think it is already here, while others pin their hopes on the turn of the millennium. The majority seem to favour a gradual dawning lasting about a century and ending around 2060. All need to be challenged with the real new age.

Know about God's new age

As Christians, we have the good news that there is to be 'a new heaven and a new earth' and that Jesus Christ is coming back again to reign (Rev 11:15; 21:1f). More than that, we shall reign with him on the new earth (Rev 5:10). And that's not all! God's new age will surpass anything that Gaia has on offer, for not only will man be changed but even the enemies of nature will be reconciled, allowing a little child to play safely in the midst of lambs, lions and leopards (Is 11:6ff).

There are still more new age benefits. There will be no more wars, and arsenals and weapons will be turned into farming tools (Is 2:4; Hos 2:18). Tears will be forgotten, death itself will die, and pain will be an empty word with no meaning (Rev 21:4). There is still more. The ravages of mankind — the poisons, the acid rain, the pollution, dangers of global warming, holes in the ozone layer, the scandal of disappearing rain forests — will all be repaired or replaced when God brings in a new heaven and a new earth.

Imagine all of this and then add the best news of all: the real new age is here and now for those who have become God's new citizens. We have already entered the kingdom and are in receipt of many of its benefits (Col 1:13,14). These include the following:

A new personhood

We have been made anew, and though the Holy Spirit and ourselves have not quite completed the task as yet, it is already looking good. We are made a new creation and the old has gone; we have a new family and a new life (2 Cor 5:17; Jn 1:12,13; Rom 6:4).

A new status

There is no need of a hundred thousand lifetimes to make us fit for God. The Son of God has done all that is necessary for our salvation. Even while we were undeserving sinners, God paid the penalty for our sins and now offers us his righteousness and holiness, total forgiveness of sin, a place in his family and all this without charge or accusation (Jn 3:16; Rom 5:8; 6:10; Heb 7:27; 10:20; Acts 4:12; Jer 31:3; Is 13:11).

A new motivation

We see our role clearly as we watch a disintegrating world, a Middle East crisis, the ravages of AIDS and disease, and the poverty and squalor. We are to be the salt preserving and flavouring the rotting parts of society in the inner city, business and commerce, the council chambers and parliament, political parties and ecology groups. We are to be involved, caring in practical ways and applying the first-aid in the crises of living.

We are to be lights of love shining out into the darkness of witchcraft and satanism, prostitution and crime, the psychic and the paranormal. We are to be in the horror, yet not of it; envoys of God's kingdom bringing spiritual light and practical love into the dark hatred that haunts society and the soul (Mt 5:13–16; 2 Cor 5:20).

A new foundation

While New Agers stand on icebergs of truth which are here today and gone tomorrow, Christians stand on the Rock of ages, and the supreme God is the very ground of our being (Ps 31:3; 62:2; 89:26; Acts 17:28).

For those readers who are content to accept the above points, feel free to move on to the next. For the more inquisitive and adventurous who want to stretch their minds a little, join me on a journey back to the lands of make-believe and madness.

Society has frequently tried to discover rock-solid truth apart from an eternal God. In the sixteenth century, René Descartes decided to doubt every possible facet of life until he arrived at a basic principle acceptable to all. He even doubted whether or not he himself existed, until finally, after days sitting by the kitchen stove, he cooked up what he believed to be an unshakeable, self-evident proof.

'I think, therefore I am,' he concluded in one of those 'eureka' moments of life. On that basis, he carefully built his philosophy.

Some spoil-sport thinkers later came and knocked it all down and ruled that this conclusion was no proof of existence. It simply affirmed his existence in some form or other. For instance, those who called themselves solipsists even went to the extent of saying that the world and everybody in it was just a figment of imagination. Nobody existed, just them and their thoughts. Come to that, only one solipsist existed because all the others were also dream actors in his mind.

These mental gymnastic gems will help you understand why philosophers today are like they are. There is nothing like a trip down Absurdity Lane to send the mind into idiotic somersaults. Whenever man relies on pure reason and logic to discover his foundations, he discovers the awful truth: there is no reason for reason itself. This needs a little explaining.

Man has pursued logic to its bitter end on rare occasions, and each time has found himself in a cul-de-sac of madness and irrationality. One or two thinkers have dallied at the end to produce something called nihilism (nothing exists, and if it did there is no logical way of proving that it exists). This idea dates back to fifth-century Greece. The last main thinker to adopt it was Friedrich Nietzsche (pronounced 'Neecher'), and you may not be too surprised to learn that it sowed the seeds of World War Two.

Nietzsche used nihilism to dismantle Christianity and make way for his own theories. Evolution told Nietzsche that man had not fallen from a super Garden of Eden status made in the divine image. That, he concluded, was the goal of man. The human being was destined to be a superman capable of mastering his own environment. The Nazis actually saw a New Age made up of a master race of tall, blond Aryans thanks in part to Nietzsche. They gladly embraced his ideas and adapted them for their own propaganda, despite the fact that insanity was diagnosed and he was committed to an asylum.

Madness was, and still is, the address at the end of the avenue of human reason and most of history's thinkers have wisely retraced their steps to establish (by faith!) some basis and purpose for existence.

Perhaps the sceptics were the most durable residents at the end of this cul-de-sac. They were as peace-loving and hippy-go-lucky as any New Ager, and all they wanted was serenity (*arataxia*), believing that nothing was absolutely certain and so no choices could be made. They merely suspended judgement and 'determined to determine nothing' — history's first drop-outs! As a movement, they found that they were going nowhere, which was not too surprising since none could decide where to go. It must have been an enormous problem, for example, deciding who was to do the washing-up after meals. When the pure sceptic was asked whether or not he wanted an after-dinner cigar, he was obliged to mumble, 'Maybe, and maybe not.'

Something had to be decided if total paralysis of life was to be averted. The first decision was for each individual to live as seemed best to himself (doesn't that have a familiar New Age ring?). Immediately the decision was taken, the sceptics realised they were undone! Horror of horrors, they had actually decided something! In a compromise, it was agreed (yet another decision) that man could no more remain suspended in mental space than he could fly.

Modern thinkers have also had their flights of fancy and many are still circling as I write. In the nineteenth century, The Romantics were the exact opposite of the pessimistic sceptics. However, their idealistic view of humanity got lost somewhere in the muddy, bloody horror of the Somme trenches. It left a post-war meaningless vacuum, peopled by the vapid flappers of the Roaring Twenties who danced to forget. In the emptiness, man was declared to be 'a bubble aimlessly floating through a purposeless universe'.[1] He had come from nowhere, he was going nowhere in particular, he just existed for the moment. This is the core of Existentialism.

But man cannot stay for long here at the end of the avenue of madness. He always retreats and erects his own staging-post by faith somewhere that suits him. Modern New Agers have retreated to idealism, believing that humanity is about to break through to a new and higher level, despite little or no reason or evidence for this claim. Of course, if they don't stick with their pipe-dream, there are only two alternatives remaining. They can stay in the cul-de-sac of madness: a world without purpose. Or they can transfer to the narrow way that originates and culminates in an eternal Almighty Creator God. Before choosing this last option, they would, of course, have to surrender their New Age independence.

Madness, make-believe or the majesty of God: the hardest decision of all for modern humanity.

A new attitude

The New Ager looks to an uncertain future: Gaia, the goddess of earth, might shrug weary mankind off her flanks; there may be a hundred thousand lifetimes to endure; the next life might be better or worse than the present one; salvation is in a Christ figure who contradicts himself so much in various human forms that he seems to need a saviour himself. It is truly amazing that New Agers retain their loving, cheerful exteriors. Underneath, as I found with some, they are a seething mass of discontent.

In complete contrast, Jesus tenderly gathered his disciples around him and told them he was going ahead to prepare Eternity for them. He would then return, for he was 'the way, the truth and the life' for them to follow. He promised them his Holy Spirit to be an ongoing guide and counsellor, a Comforter who would make his home with them. In view of all this, he understandably added, 'Peace I leave with you; my peace I give you. I do not give to you as the world gives. Do not let your hearts be troubled and do not be afraid' (Jn 14:27).

It is an attitude of peace, security and acceptance that passes all human understanding.

We are in the new age, and there is much more to come!

Give credit where it is due

Let us be honest in our approach to New Agers — and generous. True, we have highlighted New Age problems and dangers, but there is the positive flip-side which should not be lightly dismissed.

A new spiritual openness

The greatest enemy of Christianity is not a cult, not the devil, nor even the modern lions of persecution. Apathy is the number one killer. God-talk is fine if you are 'pro' or 'anti' but merely a bore for the indifferent. Inner inertia — the modern plague within materialists who care only for the external ornaments of life — is on the retreat with the dawning of a New Age. Spirituality is back on the menu of conversation and we can now discuss Jesus and the inner life with relative ease in many quarters. Of course, the battle for hearts and minds is still with us. Our Saviour is merely being transformed from a society swear-word to a cosmic Christ, but at the very least there is new interest.

Do allow the New Age some credit for bringing spirituality on to society's agenda; this is certainly a step in the right direction.

A new green interest

Here, I tread with care. A throw-away line in my last book incited strong reaction from a Christian ecologist. I had made the point that New Agers believed that all life was one and I posed the question that if God was in everything, then why not worship everything?

'New Agers generally think this is a good idea,' I wrote. 'Mother Earth must be served, hence the explosion in ecology groups and green parties...'[2]

Graham from Sheffield sent me the Christian Ecology Party introductory leaflet,[3] pointing out, 'In Sheffield there are more Christians in the Green Party than New Agers. It is true that a small minority of people have joined the Green Party because of pagan beliefs, but to say that this is the only reason is very far from the truth.'

That was not my meaning, but that apart, Graham's main point is good news — Christians taking the lead in green issues! Some Christians have interpreted the 'dominion-rulership' command of Genesis 1:28 as a charter for exploitation, forgetting the qualifying 'take care of it' text of Genesis 2:15.

Before leaving this point, Christians need to keep all their biblical wits about them in green company. For green language sounds like the Christian language but with a shorter vocabulary. It doesn't say as much. Green vision extends in the same direction as the Christian vision but, again, it stops short. It suffers from spiritual short-sightedness! It sees the creation but rarely acknowledges the Creator. Greens see the problem but not a practical solution. They appeal for man to stop sinning and killing the planet. The whole Christian reality is that man cannot stop himself being a sinner and he needs God as his Saviour.

'Green politics — politics as if people mattered,' writes

ecology evangelist and former Green Party spokesman, David Icke. 'That's the only way to save our souls.'[4]

Television's David Attenborough insists that the earth's 'continued survival now rests in our hands'.[5]

If this is the whole truth, then we are indeed lost. Thank God it isn't!

Other plusses

New Agers are saying useful things about depth in relationships and communication. We certainly need this for an age that is retreating in mobile capsules to mortgaged capsules in which entertainment is encapsulated in a plastic impersonal box.

There is also more than a grain of truth in the New Age masculine-feminine issue. Men certainly need to be less macho and more sensitive, though perhaps not as much as the new, wet, leaderless male figure that is emerging from some New Age groups.

Finally, New Agers have given love a new chance in a dark world, though some do tend to be in love with love rather than with a loving God.

As we talk with New Agers, we can allow them, among others, part of the credit for helping mankind to rediscover, or give new emphasis to, these issues. They can also provide New Agers and Christians with common ground on which to stand as they communicate with each other.

17. How to Help Ourselves

Remember Morph, the plasticine model, twisted and contorted to make a teatime television audience chuckle?

For me, it was always a modern parable of what is continually happening to mankind, with unseen fingers reaching down to manipulate the human mind first one way and then another. The last generation has been squeezed into a materialistic mould and this present age is now being measured up for the New Age multi-matrix of spirituality, love, psychic powers and peace.

The Bible, ever relevant even hundreds of years after completion, warns against the hidden pressures:

1 *The world*: 'Do not conform any longer to the pattern of this world, but be transformed by the renewing of your mind' (Rom 12:2).

2 *The flesh*: 'Watch and pray so that you will not fall into temptation. The spirit is willing but the body [flesh] is weak' (Mt 26:41).

3 *The devil*: 'Be self-controlled and alert. Your enemy the devil prowls around like a roaring lion looking for someone to devour' (1 Pet 5:8).

Protect yourself

The biblical answer to this three-pronged attack is Paul's military exhortation in Ephesians chapter 6.

However, at the risk of sounding heretical, forget the armour of God for a few minutes. You and I and the Christian church in general need to come to terms with one pressure that we are not coping with very well — fear! One whiff of a ouija board in somebody's testimony and some Christians run the proverbial mile, and it is making me and its victims weep with frustration. If I was communicating verbally at this moment, I would want to shout this warning from the roof tops: CHRISTIANS, GET YOUR ACT TOGETHER IN CARING FOR NEW AGE AND OCCULT VICTIMS.

I know of several converted New Agers and occultists who wish they had never testified to their past.

'I was proud of God and what he had done,' said Jane, an ex-wicca and former New Ager. 'But now the church just don't want to know me. They don't understand and they're scared.'

I have heard something similar dozens of times in the weeks and months before writing this chapter. Some Christians, it seems, are just so insecure in their standing with God, and so fearful of what the devil might do, that they give more glory to Satan than even practising occultists do.

Where have the good, old-fashioned biblical doctrines of assurance, victory and protection gone in Christianity today? Why do Christians no longer realise that they are safe in God's hands; that Satan can do nothing against them without God's permission (read Job's story); and that if the devil does move against those that love God, then it will be for their own good in the long run (Rom 8:28)?

And how dare we give such glory to the devil by

· shaking in our shoes at the mere mention of occult involvement and paraphernalia? How dare we elevate the occult above other sins? Do we shake with fear at adultery? Or lying? Or cheating? They are just as bad, and just as much of the devil.

And how dare we elevate the ministry to those in the occult above any other ministries? There is no difference in status between evangelism and deliverance. Both are attacking the devil's domain. There is no difference between being a church warden or church elder and being an exorcist. Both are functions of Christian ministry and equally against the devil's interests. Why do we treat occult things and New Age paraphernalia as something special?

It is time the Christian church came to its senses and viewed the New Age, paganism and the occult in a sober, balanced and mature light. Yes, we need to know what we are doing in this ministry, but so does a church warden in his own sphere! Of course we need to know whatever the ministry. But please, please, please let us stop treating the occult as something spectacular, sensational and reserved only for the chosen few ministers. Let us all roll up our sleeves and get involved, because society is; and we need to be prepared and protected by an assurance of God's almighty personal presence in this area.

All authors should be allowed one emotionally-charged outburst, and this has been mine. Now we can return to Ephesians chapter 6 and the whole armour of God.

The belt of truth (v 14)

Living in the New Age is like running a marathon in an ankle-length nightshirt. There are too many loose ideas and concepts flapping in so many winds of change, and too often I meet bruised and battered New Agers who have again tripped over them and fallen flat on their faces. We need to be wrapped around with God's word so that the biblical bonds of certainty, which harness, shape and contain life, can hold us together and enable us to act with God's freedom and speed.

The breastplate of righteousness (v 14)

New Age men and women are assured that they are fine in their present state, but there are still higher levels of consciousness to be attained. There is still a way to go before they are right — a hundred thousand lifetimes, or thereabouts. We need to remind ourselves continuously that we wear the breastplate, not of self-righteousness, but of Christ's righteousness. No matter how many attempts at life we have, we will remain sinners. More lives simply means more sins for which we need to answer. Our only righteousness is that given to us by Jesus Christ (cf Rom 6:10; Heb 7:27).

Foot protection (v 15)

New Agers pride themselves on being people of peace, and yet, when New Age friends have opened up in moments of intimacy, they appear to be cowering, vulnerable figures in a war zone minefield. They tread fearfully through imaginary successive lifetimes, without any protection or assurance of future security. I cry for them and would love them to follow in the footsteps of a heavenly Father whose way of salvation and victory over the enemy affords full protection, and a peace that passes all understanding; a peace which the world cannot give (cf Phil 4:6,7; Jn 14:27).

The shield of faith (v 16)

The Roman shield of which Paul is thinking when writing to the Ephesians is not the small, round dustbin-lid type with a nob in the middle. It is a multi-layered chunk of protection, the size of a door. The fiery darts of the enemy were easily absorbed by the door and extinguished. There are many darts which can penetrate and damage the Christian as he comes near the New Age. Talk of Gaia and God, of relationships and of love, of Christ figures — all these can pierce a simple faith and can mislead. Our faith in Jesus Christ needs to be layered with all the historical evidence of Christianity, weighty biblical material and an all-enveloping relationship with Jesus Christ.

The helmet of salvation (v 17)

The mind of man is wooed; it is manipulated; the consciousness is altered. The New Age mind-engineers are for ever dreaming up new techniques and methods to empty the head and fill it with the refuse of the East, the occult or the paranormal. The Christian's protection is in the Holy Spirit's constant renewing of the mind, and the refusal to be conformed to the surrounding world (cf Rom 12:2).

A two-edged sword (v 17)

The Roman sword had both edges sharpened, for attack and defence. Yes, we need to be soaked in God's word so that we can have a ready defence against New Age ideas. But we also need to care enough to go on the attack and try to win New Agers for God. With all the love and sensitivity that God gives to us, we need to apply the Good News cleanly and accurately to cut away the wire wool and mesh that entraps New Agers.

Helpful contacts

Christian Response to the Occult, PO Box 150, Bromley, Kent (Counselling and literature — particularly good leaflet on the New Age)

Reachout Trust, Alpha Place, Garth Road, Morden, Surrey SM4 4LX (Offering literature, resource data bank, advice and counselling)

Christian Publicity Organisation, Garcia Estate, Canterbury Road, Worthing, W Sussex BN13 1BW (Excellent New Age leaflet — CP0837)

Evangelical Alliance, Whitefield House, 186 Kennington Park Road, London SE11 4BT ('New Age Problem. Age-old Problem' — good quality, eight-page, A4 brochure)

Cult Information Centre, BCM Cults, London WC1 N3X (Focuses on prevention through education. Gives talks on cults and the New Age and provides various materials)

18. The Last Word

Our story has been about people; deliberately so. It could have been a cold theological analysis of a new change in our age and culture, but that would have been to miss out the people who are at least as important.

We needed to meet Jenny and Tom, Dr Bloom, even Eileen Caddy and Sir George Trevelyan and the others. We needed to know their beliefs; to understand why they are as they are and to feel for them as flesh and blood people. I wanted you to care, and perhaps look out for them down your street.

Too often we caricature those whom we consider our enemies, and it hurts them. It also damages any chances of evangelism and it tears the God of truth apart. To ensure that you had as accurate a view of the New Age as possible, a copy of this book's original manuscript was sent to Findhorn for comments. Findhorn's critic, Stan Stanfield, made a number of factual corrections and sent the following letter with the returned manuscript:

> I enjoyed reading your book. I felt you were quite fair
> in your presentation, without either compromising
> your beliefs or misrepresenting those of New Agers.
> Just one point: I think you will find that most New

Agers accept an incredible, awesome and loving
'Mind' behind what we know as reality. Certainly, I
don't worship the creation and ignore the Creator. I
think therein lies the best basis for agreement
between Christians and New Agers. Certainly, we can
learn something from each other, in the ongoing
process of communication.

Only as we meet the people can we hope to understand
where they truly are. In seeing them, we can also identify
others who might live along our road.

They are there: the alternative family with Mum
preparing 'veggie burgers', Dad hooked on Gaia and
canvassing for the Green Party. The kids in one
neighbourhood I knew used to swap crystals instead of
soccer cards, or dowse for hidden treasure with rods and
psychic pendulums. You are not likely to meet such
extremes, but there is Aunty Anne who reads the tea-
leaves and won't make a decision without consulting the
natal horoscope prescribed by the family astrologer. And
don't forget the neighbour who is so superstitious that she
keeps a spare supply of salt to toss over her shoulder to
ward off disaster.

Perhaps the neighbour you know is simply sick of an
age of possessions and hypocrisy and yearns for
something new, trying to fill the gaping inner void in his
life. He's imprisoned in mortgaged suburbia, at the mercy
of a rickety family banger which thinks it is a ravenous
caterpillar devouring the expensive leaves in his wallet.
He may never have heard of the New Age movement. To
him, Findhorn may be as remote as Timbucktoo and not
half so interesting. But all this aside, he is spiritually
seeking, open to all ideas, dabbling in alternative
remedies and life styles and maybe even into the fringe
playthings of the occult. The New Age has crept into his

life in the same way that it is seeping into our culture and along our streets — without announcement.

Our great need today is to understand what is happening in the minds of our friends and neighbours so that we can help them. It is my prayer that this book will go a little way towards this end.

Appendix
Medicine for the New Age

'This is the New Age of healing and wholeness,' a Glastonbury New Ager tells me. 'The old ways are not working. This is the age of alternatives.'

Nearby, a young woman sits cross-legged in the Buddha position while a friend called Ysan strokes the air around her body.

'This is holistic intuitive massage,' the stroker explains. (Other practitioners I know call it Ch'i Kung, Quigong or Ch'i gong.)

'It is basically manipulating and focusing the energy in the body,' explains Ysan, a twenty-year-old student who has joined 120,000 others on the Alternative Green Ecology fields at the town's Festival of Contemporary Performing Arts. 'It's getting in tune with the person you're trying to heal and just letting your hands feel where they are meant to go. It is a gift which has been given to me.'

'By whom?' I ask.

'From Gaia, the earth goddess.' (Other practitioners give the credit to Mother Earth, or a supreme overseeing being, or the cosmic forces, or the power of divinity which is 'deep down and within each of us'.)

'It feels great!' the patient breaks in. 'I feel much more whole. Ysan is brilliant, you should try one.'

And why not?

Not my reaction, you understand. But it is the response increasingly of the ordinary man or woman in the street. They might perhaps feel one degree under, or have chronic complaints that have defeated the best that orthodox medicine can offer. They are suffering people with no particular strong world-views either one way or the other and...

'What the heck!' they hear themselves exclaiming. 'What have we to lose?'

The answer to that question is at the heart of the matter, especially as Princess Diana and other royalty and celebrities lead more and more of the public through the increasingly respected portals of alternative medicine.[1] So many parts of society are producing so many different answers that the medical establishment, the British Medical Association, has now launched a large-scale investigation into alternative therapies.[2] More than ever before, GPs and health clinics are showing an active interest in alternative treatments while, at the same time, many orthodox practitioners worry that fringe medicine patients may be suffering untold damage because they are not getting proper care.

Dorothy, for example, was treated for jaundice symptoms but hepatitis tests proved negative. Doctors investigated and concluded that the likely cause was a two-year herbal treatment involving the drug Valerian. The Department of Health's Committee on the Safety of Medicines registered ten other similar cases in the six years up to 1990. One patient had died. A study in north-east England and Scotland highlighted similar question marks over the drug. The British Herbal Medicines Association claimed that there was 'no proof that Valerian has any hepatoxicity'.[3] The matter remains unresolved.

Meanwhile, there continues to be concern about potent

herbal drugs being freely available in the high street without the need of a doctor's prescription. (More happily in America herbal medicines are required to meet the same criteria as drugs.) Manufacturers never make claims on the labels of their herbal products and so avoid the need to licence them under the Medicines Act. They are therefore sold in health or New Age outlets regardless of potency and without controls and the retailers are able to make verbal claims culled from the wholesalers' herbal manuals. Less charitable critics believe this is a deliberate marketing ploy for a multi-million pound alternative industry.

The possible physical dangers are only one area of concern. Many coming from a Christian perspective are suggesting that there are also spiritual risks in this health care for the New Age.

At one end of the Christian spectrum is Dr Douglas Calcott, who states, 'Satan is desperate to deceive us on this issue and has raised up many counterfeit physicians and methods of treatment.'[4]

New Age author Roy Livesey writes 'an exposé of the occult explosion in holistic healing' and publishes a 'plea for discernment' in his book *Understanding Alternative Medicine*.[5]

At the other end of the Christian perspective are active believers and practitioners of alternative medicine, one of whom I have quoted in the coming section on acupuncture. In between the extremes are questioning voices, like those of Paul and Teri Reisser and John Weldon, authors of *New Age Medicine*:

> The authors examine the roots of holistic health and many of its therapies, revealing New Age influence and Eastern mysticism which undergird so much of the movement...This book outlines principles that

> anyone can use to evaluate whether or not to
> undergo unusual health therapies...[6]

For those who wish to go beyond this quick glance over the field of alternative medicine, I warmly commend the above book.

A brief, alphabetical and by no means comprehensive guide of New Age medicine will help us at this stage. Please take in the information about these therapies as you wish. Feel free to digest them now in one sitting or simply bypass them until you need to know more about individual treatments. Whatever you choose to do, try to take in the 'Dos and Don'ts' of fringe medicine on the last couple of pages.

I have met the following treatments at Findhorn and Glastonbury, and at various New Age, psychic and body, mind and soul festivals. Many of these treatments have now graduated from the fringe into mainstream society, such as NHS and private hospitals, clinics, local surgeries and health shops. There are more than a hundred separate alternative medicine therapies now available. I shall dwell on the most popular treatments, and mention some of the others with a short description.

Acupuncture

Energy (or ch'i) is said to flow through a dozen or so main channels (meridians) in the body. It is claimed that needles inserted and vibrated (or pressures applied) at various points control the flow, bringing pain relief, draining excesses of energy or restoring deficiencies. Acupuncture was introduced into the fringes of Western culture by pre-war French researchers, but it was not until after US President Nixon's China visit that it really caught Western imaginations.

Major operations involving wide-awake acupuncture patients were filmed after China was opened up to outsiders. The authenticity of these has since been questioned[7] but there is no doubt that acupuncture does have some anaesthetic qualities. Some medics have attributed this to auto-suggestion or the placebo effect (the patient's confidence in the technique or practitioner). To be fair, those immune to suggestion, such as babies and animals, are also affected by acupuncture. Other medics argue that natural, morphine-like substances (enkephalins and endorphins) are released, while a large school of thought opts for the 'gate theory'. This suggests that irritation by needles at special points (between 365 and 800 needle or pressure points, depending on whom you listen to) can close off the pathways along which pain messages are carried to the brain.[8] The number of possible gates has ranged from one to a countless number.[9] There are other neurological explanations and some researchers persuasively suggest that hypnosis is the real answer.

Dr Tony Bambridge, in his book *Acupuncture Investigated*, concludes his scientific and historical survey by expressing the fears which are present among some Christians:

> The Yellow Emperor and the ensuing band of Taoist luminaries who started up and raised acupuncture to the status we see it now were all involved in varying degrees of spiritualism, sorcery or divination; practices which are an abomination to God...Therefore the principles of ch'i and yang, meridians and sticking needles in special points are ungodly (perhaps one could say, demonically inspired: 1 Tim 4:1).[10]

There are Christian doctors who strongly contest this. They insist that they have set aside the 'mumbo-jumbo' of the East and merely extracted the techniques which, though unexplainable, are useful and beneficial. One Christian doctor spoke to me at length as to why she had devoted her whole practice to acupuncture in the context of preventive medicine. With refreshing honesty and patience, she explained its virtues and mysteries and also elaborated on possible explanations of how acupuncture worked. At the end, her honesty caused her to add: 'There's a lot we don't know about how it works — a lot physiologically. And we don't know why it works better in some people than with others. I find it works best with children and little old ladies...It does puzzle me why it varies from person to person. There are probably lots of chemical things going on that we haven't discovered yet. There is a lot of work to be done, but I think, in the years to come, acupuncture will be taught in medical schools because it's a very useful tool.'

Some doctors would be disturbed to find acupuncture heading this brief survey of fringe medicines. They would insist that it has earned its place in orthodoxy, especially when the current Princess of Wales has acupuncture sessions at her London health and fitness club. Others, as we have seen, disagree.

To this all-too-brief assessment of the acupuncture arguments needs to be added the principles set out at the end of this appendix. Similar comments apply to acupressure, which comprises a mixture of acupuncture and massage.

Aromatherapy

This treatment relies on inhaling the fragrances of herbs, oils and spices. It does not sound too fantastic when we remember that most of us have spent a spluttering half-hour over a bowl of Friars Balsam on the kitchen table with a towel draped over the head. Aromatherapists, however, go a little further by suggesting that we take in through inhalation the essence and energy of the herbs to keep us going.

Aurasomatherapy

This treatment rests on the belief that an electromagnetic field or 'aura' surrounds the body. '*Soma*' relates to the being within the body. The therapy therefore aims to balance the two to create health and wellbeing. This was the intention of Vicky Wall, who invented the therapy between the two World Wars. She was the seventh child of a seventh child with healing, psychic and clairvoyant gifts which were developed after three near-death experiences. The therapy today involves the use of herbal extracts and essential oils and is a type of colour therapy (see below).

Bach flower remedies

Fifty years after Dr Edward Bach's death, the New Age has rejuvenated his treatments based on the process of 'potentising' plants, herbs and flowers. Even the morning dew is believed to extract the essence of the plants on which it rests, due to the action of sunlight on it.

To 'potentise' a plant means to dilute its essence to such an extent that hardly a molecule of the original remains. This is the foundation principle of homoeopathy (see below). Success in treatment relies on the energy infused in the diluted solution and owes nothing to any possible curative effect of the plant.

Bio-therapies

This is my name for a family of techniques in which a person's life (from the Greek *bios*) or life-force are manipulated and managed.

1   *Biofeedback* is the process of measuring involuntary bodily functions, via electrical monitoring equipment, and then using techniques like yoga to gain more control over them. A measuring device can, for example, be attached to the body and the read-out given in the form of a musical note or tone. The patient observes which actions, thoughts or positions affect the tone and he can then 'feed back' in the appropriate thoughts and actions to bring about the required adjustment to the tone. Meditation, relaxation, yoga, hypnosis and various other alternative techniques are used to create the required calming actions and thoughts.

2   *Bioenergetics* involves freeing the life-energy from the blocks of past traumas. People, it is claimed, live at such a low energy level that they never reach their full potential. Through breathing exercises, movement and free self-expression a person is taught to escape from the bondages of upbringing and freed to be an unfettered spirit.

3   *Biorhythms* is a system that insists that the physical, emotional and intellectual sides of life undulate in rhythms of between twenty-three and thirty-three days. This has become so popular that you can now plug your patterns into your own personal computer or electronic or mechanical biorhythm calculators and check how your cycles are doing. We need to note at this point that medical science has, of course, identified and verified various bodily rhythms, and every woman has to resign herself to her monthly rhythm. Each of us also has a circadian (daily) rhythm which the jet-setting (and-

lagging) crowd know only too well. The alternative bio-rhythms, however, are by no means universally attested, and seem to owe more to guessology than either biology or physiology.

Bodywork

This is a general New Age term covering all those therapies used to develop a more psychologically and physically healthy body. Many listed in this survey would come under this heading.

Chiropractic

This is the creation of Dr Daniel Palmer, who suggested that all disease was caused by misalignments (or sub-luxations) in the spine. Manipulation, acupuncture, reflexology and similar treatments were prescribed. Osteopathy was developed earlier, and involves different forms of manipulation.

Colour therapy

All recognise that colour affects us to a certain extent. It is more pleasant, for instance, to walk into a light, pastel-tinted room than a dingy hovel with dark brown rust for wallpaper. Colour therapy insists that the whole of life and its moods are governed by the contents of the rainbow. Some people even use colour preferences to diagnose a future employee's psychological make-up. While conventional medicine colours anti-depressants red deliberately to increase the patient's subjective response, colour therapy enters the alternative medicine field when it insists that blues lower your blood pressure and reds do the opposite, and so on.

Crystals

I spent half an hour interviewing Ken in his tepee on Glastonbury's festival fields, while at the same time watching him treat a patient under his electrocrystal machine. He was like a boy with a new toy, having just bought it for £2,000. It consisted of a 4ft x 6in wooden board, suspended over the patient. At various intervals on the underside were embedded different coloured crystals to correspond with the patient's seven chakras. Chakras are the energy centres said to exist in the human aura: base of spine; genitals; navel; solar plexus; heart; throat; eyes and crown of head. The whole board and its multicoloured crystals were wired up to a twelve-volt car battery.

The structure and texture of crystals has fascinated man from the dawn of time because they seem to contain light and energy. Shamans, witches, psychics and now New Agers utilise them to feed energy into the body and correct the energy that is said to be already there.

Homeopathy

This was laughed out of eighteenth-century society shortly after Samuel Hahnemann introduced his theory that 'like cures like'; that an infinitesimal amount of a dangerous or disease-provoking substance could actually bring healing and health. Hahnemann himself believed that spiritual powers made the substance more active. He began experimenting with poisons, and diluted them so much that there was practically not a molecule of the original remaining in the final solution. He called this process 'potentising' (see Bach flower remedies for definition), and believed that the preparations stimulated the body to marshal its own reserves of power and healing.

Iridology

Iridology is the diagnosis of a person's health by examining the pigmented centre of the eye. Parts of the iris are thought to correspond to the various organs of the body and coloured photographs of the eye can therefore reveal the body's health or lack of it, so it is claimed. Scientific tests, however, have proved very discouraging but the New Age public still like the concept.

Massage

This can mean anything from a light stroke of the air around the body (as seen at the beginning of this appendix) to the near grievous bodily harm of Rolphing, when extreme pressure is used to realign muscles said to be frozen by stress. Within these extremes there is therapeutic massage as performed by qualified physiotherapists.

Psychic surgery/healing

The Time and the Place television presenter Mike Scott shared with me the horror he felt after returning from the Philippines to show a television audience his programme on psychic surgery. 'Surgeons' who appeared to be in a trance were seen removing liver-like slivers of tissue from a blood-covered, unopened stomach.

'The switchboard was jammed for hours afterwards,' he told me. 'We heard of dozens of people trying to book air flights for themselves and their sick relatives. We had no alternative but to go back and do an exposé of the whole sorry business.'[11]

Some 'psychic healing' has been exposed as a sham.

Specimens allegedly removed from patients in the East have been found to be chicken livers.

Sleight of hand apart, psychic healing involves the channelling of spiritual and psychic power from the healer into the individual. Many alternative therapies involve the healer transferring some of his surplus energy into the patient, who is thought deficient in his power to fight against an illness or disease.

Radionics

Also called radiesthesia or dowsing. It is the theory that the body radiates an energy field, and that by dowsing with a pendulum a practitioner should be able to detect varying strengths in the energy given off. Weak radiations would suggest tissue damage or disease.

Reflexology

As sometimes seen on TV soap operas, like *Neighbours*, when characters are seen to massage each other's feet. It involves the belief that each zone of the foot corresponds to a particular part of the body and that massage of the foot can release the imbalances of energy in affected areas. When organs or muscles are unhealthy, it is thought that they cause crystalline deposits to form under the skin of the relevant foot zones. Reflexologists believe that massage can alleviate the problem. How the foot zones are linked to the respective parts of the body is anybody's guess. They bear no relation to any neurological pathways. Reflexology can also involve the palms of the hands as well as the soles of the feet.

Shiatsu

This Japanese word means 'finger pressure' and the treatment involves an elaborate, all-over body massage with finger tips. It is similar in theory to acupressure.

Zone therapy

This is a form of reflexology and is similar in some ways to acupressure. It involves massaging certain surface zones of the body to affect vital organs, muscles and tissues.

A Christian response

Alternative medicine presents us with a choice of reactions. We could simply dismiss the whole scene as diabolically satanic, as do some Christians, or willingly embrace it, as do other Christians. We could opt for wise caution and go the middle way, which accepts the known and tested and holds the unknown at a safe distance. Personally, I have my own list of DOs and DON'Ts which you might find useful:

1   **Do** be wary of the energy experts, those who promise to manipulate invisible, unknown, unidentified, unexplained fields or streams of power in the body. It is your physical, emotional and spiritual health they are playing around with in their ignorance.

2   **Do** be wary of the God called One: the idea that God or the universal force or the cosmic universal energy is coursing through everything from the kitchen sink to your big toe. All is not one. God, the ultimate in power and

energy, is within and yet apart and totally separate from his creation.

3   **Do** avoid the psychic souls who delve into the depths of the occult and dredge up a dubious spiritual solution to cure your acne. They will be very sincere and probably quite delightful people, trying their utmost to bring you comfort and solace. I have had to minister to their patients afterwards and it has not been spiritually all that pleasant, either for them or me.

4   **Don't** touch the exclusive types, those who refuse to share their secret therapy with others. Every medical discovery in orthodox medicine is openly shared, and always has been, for the general benefit of mankind, after sufficient testing. Those who want to keep their therapies under wraps have their own welfare closer to heart than yours or mine.

5   **Do** ask questions and insist on comprehensible answers. If the practitioner is not able to make you understand with reasonable ease, he either does not know what he is doing, or he does, and he's trying to make sure you don't. Beware the peddlers of gobbledygook!

6   **Don't** gamble with your health by allowing untrained hands within an arm's length of your body. It has always seemed reasonable to me to examine the practitioner before he does the same to me. Should the certificates hanging in the waiting-room be signed by the principal of a remote, unknown university or faculty, I generally take my body elsewhere. This nugget of wisdom was learned in just one hard lesson. I had spent a week on my knees repairing and repainting my trusty but rusty banger. I felt

something go in my right knee on the third day. By Friday, the day before our summer holidays began, the pain was so bad that I went to an osteopath who gave me acupuncture and a heavy massage. By the time he had finished, I was fit only for casualty, where an X-ray showed a chipped knee-cap!

Painful lessons I never repeat.

7 **Do** beware of the simpering, ingratiating healer. Note the professional attitude of your GP as he offers you his expertise, learning and wisdom. He may have a lousy bedside manner, but one thing you rarely find is a doctor touting for customers. When you do come across one, it raises questions.

8 **Do** ignore testimonials. If a healer has to stoop to other people's stories of alleged success, he is generally hard-up for proper evidence. Patients' feelings of wellness are notoriously fickle, and it often depends on when they wrote such testimonials. Surveys in this area reveal that some patients wrote their words of praise prematurely.

9 **Do** beware of those who believe that there is no alternative but alternative medicine. It is true that orthodox medicine has been its own worst enemy at times. It has relied too heavily on drug treatments that have done more harm than good; it has not too successfully coped with stress and psychosomatic illnesses; it has rarely had time for patients beyond administering a brief tickle with a cold stethoscope; and some patients have not even survived the waiting-list, let alone the treatment. However, the overworked, underappreciated local GP is not without his successes and many of us would not even be alive today without his skill. The doctor may be hazardous to health on

occasions, but it still makes the headlines when proved. And that means it is still rare!

10 **Do** remember the real you when it comes to treatment. Beyond the skinful of bones and grisly bits there lies the spiritual. It's a poor bargain when the bad back gets straightened at the expense of a bent spirit. What does it profit a back sufferer if he gains his whole height yet loses his soul in the process? Watch your world-view! A God-centred sanity can so easily be replaced by an off-centre god.

11 **Do** consider the origins of your treatment. If it came from an occultic, spiritist or Eastern mystical background, do make further enquiries before accepting it as good. It may well be all right; after all, not all discoveries of orthodox medicine came from saints. However, dubious origins should prompt a question or two.

12 **Do** remember that we do have other alternatives to the alternative scene. When you get to the end of orthodox medicine, and preferably well before that, recall that we have a God who can repair life when it goes wrong. He did after all make it in the first place. Sometimes we don't give God a chance. Try calling the elders of your church to attend you with prayer and oil (Jas 5:14,15) or go to your local healing service.

13 **Do** give Christian positive thinking a go, if your problem relates to the emotional or psychological. Opting for the secular variety might give you a superficial confidence but it will lock out God, and it will also collapse the moment life's pressures bite deeply. Then you will have nothing. See the end of Chapter 8 for a few suggestions.

14 **Do** consider the roles of the world, the flesh and the devil in your illness, whether physical, psychological, emotional or spiritual. The stress and pressures of the world, the demands and urges of the flesh, and the deception and deceit of the devil need a bit more than a quivering acupuncture needle. Be especially careful when illness has a spiritual or inner origin. Delving into Eastern practices for solutions would not be the brightest of moves.

15 **Do** examine your conscience when illness strikes. No, I'm not coming out with that old wives' tale about God punishing the ungodly with plague and pestilence. But a bad conscience is notorious for playing havoc with the nerves and digestive system. There is even evidence that cancers and ulcers and mental illness can be caused by gnawing unforgiveness and resentments. We are assured of confidence and peace with God (and hopefully an absence of ulcers) when our hearts are unable to condemn us, because we are walking in the right way (1 Jn 3:21–22).

16 **Do** avoid the New Age 'name it, claim it' syndrome. Christian positive thinking dwells on one positive certainty. God likes to exercise his own will. He is not a one-armed bandit machine that automatically pays out when we put enough in. Let God be God, and let his will be done.

17 **Don't** automatically follow your leaders. Alternative medicine may seem attractive because of the involvement of royalty, or a favourite celebrity, or maybe even some church leaders. None of us is infallible. We all need to be accountable and open to questions.

18   **Do** ask yourself whether the Great Physician would be happy working alongside your choice of practitioner. If in doubt, make an excuse and leave!

Notes

Chapter 1

1 Marilyn Ferguson, *The Aquarian Conspiracy* (Paladin: London, 1980), p 18.
2 *ibid* p 26.
3 Caryl Matrisciana, *Gods of the New Age* (Harvest House: USA), book cover.
4 *ibid*
5 Constance Cumbey, *The Hidden Dangers of the Rainbow* (Huntingdon House: USA, 1983), fourth flyleaf.
6 Roy Livesey, *Understanding the New Age* (New Wine Press: Chichester, 1986), p 234.
7 Walter Martin, *The New Age Cult* (Bethany House: USA, 1989).
8 Tex Marrs, *Dark Secrets of the New Age* (Crossway: USA, 1987), back cover.
9 Two thirds of Britain's workforce has already joined a partly cashless society, with wages paid directly into the bank. A campaign continues at present to encourage the remainder to fall in line and so reduce the temptation of wage snatches and muggings. Mary Stewart Relph PhD, in her book *When Your Money Fails* (Ministries Inc: USA, 1981), warns of the collapse of the world's major currencies. Money, she reasons, will be replaced by Electronic Fund Transfer (already partly present in society), with each person having a single card and number. She outlines several experiments of placing a mark on the body to replace plastic cards. She also highlights the worldwide usage of the figures 666 (mark of

179

the Beast in the Book of Revelation). These figures are currently the entry code into the world banking system.
10   Kevin Logan, *Paganism and the Occult* (Kingsway: Eastbourne, 1988).

Chapter 2
1   Not the real name.
2   Shirley MacLaine, *Out on a Limb* (Bantam Books: London, 1983), p 209.
3   The story of Hannah came into the public domain following the inquest on her death on the 7th March, 1990. It was subsequently featured in television programmes and in newspaper articles either to support or refute claims of ritual abuse and child sacrifice.

Hannah (also known as Caroline) Marchant had been one of several dozen women and children who had come forward to give evidence of ritual child abuse and sacrifice. This evidence — much is still being received — is being collected by several child and family agencies including the NSPCC and, as I write, the appropriate authorities are investigating.

A national controversy over ritual abuse claims arose when certain groups in society began to demand evidence of a more substantial nature than the anecdotal variety. This was started by a magazine with the rather unwieldy title of the Occult Response to the Christian Response to the Occult (ORCRO). It lobbied the national media and was particularly successful with *The Independent on Sunday*. Reporter Rosie Waterhouse took up the challenge, attempting to portray the ritual-abuse claims as propaganda from evangelical fundamentalists. This was doomed to failure because evidence of abuse was coming mainly from secular child agencies and even the social services.

When Hannah's death became public, ORCRO and others associated with the magazine attempted to discredit her testimony, part of which she had set down in a half-finished manuscript. She had begun to write her story as a warning to others about the dangers of the occult.

The Independent on Sunday agreed to let two freelance journalists, David Hebditch and Nick Anning, investigate her life, and their findings were published in the magazine section on the 30th December, 1990, under the title 'A Ritual Fabrication'. Having traced out Hannah's life history, the story suggested that there was no way she could have been involved in satanic ritual abuse or sacrifice: she had never been on her own long enough to have had the baby she claimed had been kept by the satanists, nor the baby which she said had been aborted and sacrificed. The reporters concluded that she had probably made up the whole story and that she had committed suicide because of the pressure to sustain the fiction for the Christians.

As an in-depth investigation for a quality newspaper it was disappointing. There were fifteen factual errors in the first two columns of the twelve-column story, the part in which I was involved. This related to Hannah's overnight stay at my vicarage and her subsequent overdose. I spoke to three other people featured in other columns of the story and they also told me of errors relating to them. I pointed out the numerous errors in a letter to *The Independent on Sunday*. They did not print it. The new Press Commission is investigating complaints from myself and others as we go to press.

Leaving poor journalism aside, I can understand society's difficulties in accepting evidence of ritual abuse and sacrifice. I remember how difficult I found it at the beginning. It took three counselling situations before I was prepared even to consider ritual abuse as a possibility. Now, after speaking with many other women, men and children, I have no doubts that this sordid business is only too real. Once you listen to the logical and coherent accounts of these victims and perpetrators — and especially to Hannah's lucid down-to-earth story which we have on thirty hours of tape — it is far simpler to believe that they are not the product of over--emotional or deranged imaginations, but actual personal experiences.

It is our hope that the more mature members of society are able, at the very least, to listen to the cries of our hurting women and children and reach sane, helpful conclusions. Writer Andrew Boyd has thoroughly researched the question of ritual abuse in recent years and publishes his findings in *Blasphemous Rumours* (HarperCollins, London 1991).

His report on Hannah Marchant is a good corrective to the shallow investigation carried out by *The Independent on Sunday*.

Finally, as we go to press, the Department of Health has announced a two-year study of ritual abuse, which I very much welcome.

Chapter 3

1   Paul Hawken, *The Magic of Findhorn* (Fontana/Collins: Glasgow, 1975).
2   *ibid* p 156.
3   *ibid* p 118.
4   Official *Earthweek* magazine, April 1990, p 3.
5   16th August, according to ancient Aztec legend, was forecast as the end of the world. It was also the day when old Mayan and Aztec calendars converged. This was twinned with the American Hopi Indian legends which predicted doom unless 144,000 sundancers performed on this day. The Harmonic Convergence was the result, at sites like England's Glastonbury Tor, the Giant Pyramid in Egypt, Australia's Ayres Rock, California's Mount Shastra and Japan's Mount Fuji.
6   Michael Cole, *What Is the New Age?* (Hodder and Stoughton: London, 1990), p 102.
7   Elliot Miller, *A Crash Course on the New Age Movement* (Monarch: Eastbourne, 1990), p 206.
8   Eric Pement, *Consensus or Conspiracy*, p 35. (Quoted by Douglas R. Groothuis in *Unmasking the New Age*, IVP: USA, 1986.)
9   Douglas R. Groothuis, *Unmasking the New Age* (IVP: USA, 1986), p 35.

Chapter 4

1   Since Vatican II, there have been significant changes in Roman Catholicism. No longer is there a monolithic, authoritarian, one-belief structure with neat, precise beliefs on each tiny dogma. Vatican II, and meetings and

groups since, revealed quite sizeable parties within the Church, including the traditionalists (like the present Pope), modernist liberals and charismatics. My conversion experience hinged on the biblical doctrine of salvation by faith alone as opposed to salvation by faith and works, officially still held by Roman Catholics. There are changes happening. The Anglican and Roman Catholic International Congress have produced Agreed Statements on three issues, including justification. Talks go on, especially about the 'rich ambiguity of language' used in the statements. Progress is being made with still quite a distance to go.

2   The essence of truth which led to my conversion was first seen by me in the letter to the Ephesians, especially chapter 2:8,9.

Chapter 5

1   Paul Hawken, *The Magic of Findhorn* (Fontana/Collins: Glasgow, 1975), pp 121–122.

Chapter 6

1   James Lovelock's two books are Gaia: *A New Look at Life on Earth* (1982) and *The Ages of Gaia* (1988) (both Oxford University Press).

2   James Lovelock, *The Ages of Gaia,* back cover.

3   *ibid* p 217.

4   *ibid* back cover. Lovelock also writes (p 236), 'Gaia is not purposefully anti-human, but so long as we continue to change the global environment against her preferences, we encourage our replacement with more environmentally seemly species.'

   Doesn't this make you thank God that Gaia isn't God! It must be weird having a god who cares more for itself and its own than for us. Imagine the joy of New Agers when they discover that the real God loves them and the world so much that he actually gave his one and only Son to save them (Jn 3:16).

5   *ibid* back cover.

6   The laws of thermodynamics (heat and energy) dictate that after 5,000,000,000 years our planet should have gone

into cold storage long ago. Computers further calculate that in this huge span of time, the seas should show a far greater concentration of minerals, especially salt, than they do at present.

7   Molecular biologist Michael Denton has gathered together an impressive argument against the modern concepts of evolution. He has no religious axe to grind and presents himself as an honest scientist continuing to ask honest questions. See *Evolution: A Theory in Crisis* (Hutchinson Group for Burnett Books: London, 1985).

8   For nearly a century, science has struggled with Max Planck's quantum theory about the odd ways in which heat travels. He looked at other radiations and concluded that energy did not flow constantly but travelled in quanta — packets of definite amounts — rather like the dots and dashes of Morse code, as opposed to a constant tone.

As the science of quantum physics increased, so too did the number of illogicalities. Particles suddenly stopped acting like units and became wavelengths, and made unpredictable transitions or quantum leaps. The solidity of our material world was beginning to fade into flickering, insubstantial connections; matter was not so much matter as relationships between energy events. There were unknown forces at work and, though a mathematical formula existed to prove the existence of a force beyond nature (thanks to Prigogine), physicists were not inclined to accept this. They remained unsure until one of their number, J.S. Bell, made what has since been described as 'the most profound discovery of science'. He came up with what at first seemed an absurd idea, claiming that when paired particles were separated they would still behave identically. In 1964, he showed this by reversing the polarity in a separated 'twin' and demonstrating that the other particle changed polarity simultaneously. There was, it seemed, an unknown, unexplainable connection between the two, despite the divorce and separation. (This is known as Bell's Theorem.)

Quantum physics mocks the modern intellect of men and women and makes them wonder whether in fact they have come all that far from the uncertainties of their pagan past. Puny little humanity, on an insignificant planet in a corner of a galaxy that is lost in ten billion others, is just as awe-struck as its distant tribal cousins at the quirks and foibles of nature.

In our jungle-clearing days, lightning flashed and winds roared and we immediately began to placate the spirits of the air and woods. We worshipped that which we did not understand.

Yesterday, scientists discovered that the quirks and quarks of subatomic physics seem to have little or no relationship to the Newtonian laws on which the whole of modern science is based. Even the foundation principles of Einstein's physics are under threat, as mathematics 'prove' the existence of a force 'in nature' that is more than nature and has a remarkable capacity to organise itself. Today, we end up making a 'Gaia god' out of nature and planet Earth.

When will we as a species learn to suspend final judgement until more of the facts are known? Certainly, let us play with our hypotheses, and even hone them into theories and so on. But wouldn't it be marvellous if, just for once as a race, we acknowledged that we are not going to completely crack the code of a universe that was made by an almighty and incredibly complex Mind. By all means, let us carry on researching and probing, for we are committed to using our gifts and abilities to the fullest extent for the good of humanity and our own personal development. But let us do so with awareness of the fact that the puny human mind is never going to be big enough to embrace the creative intellect of God. You cannot ask a thimble to play host to an ocean.

Chapter 7

1 Robert Ogilvie Crombie, quoted by Peter Hawken, *The Magic of Findhorn* (Fontana), p 147.
2 *ibid* pp 140–143.
3 *ibid* p 144.
4 *ibid* p 145.

Chapter 8

1   Findhorn Foundation, *Guest Programme 1990 Catalogue*, p 10.

2   *ibid* p 11.

3   Chris Bourne, *21st Century* New Age article (July 1990), p 42.

4   *ibid*

5   TM has its roots in the Vedic scriptures, which are the basis of Hinduism. Theologians and interfaith experts often follow the modern theory that Christians need to discover the areas in which the Holy Spirit has been at work in heathen faiths. For many, TM is recognised as the work of God's Spirit, the line taken by some contributors in the book mentioned in the footnote below. It seems a dangerous belief, considering the numerous warnings in Scripture for Christians to avoid 'different gospels' and 'false prophets' and 'being unequally yoked with unbelievers' (Gal 1:8; Acts 13:6–11; 2 Cor 6:14). It is hardly likely that the Holy Spirit would inspire those directions in his word, and then promptly break them with his deeds. To be sure, God's Spirit is at work in the East and everywhere, but that is different from stating that he contributes to beliefs which deny the truth that he has inspired.

6   Adrian B. Smith (ed), *TM: An Aid to Christian Growth* (Mayhew McCrimmon: Essex, 1983, reprinted 1987).

7   Stuart Hall stress tape advertisement, *Observer*, 19th March 1990: p 7.

8   Official brochure, New World Company, Halesworth, Suffolk.

9   Official brochure, Lifestyle Libraries, Blandford, Dorset.

10 Richard Hittleman, *Yoga for Health* (Hamlyn: London, 1981) based on his television series of the same name.

11 Joseph Corvo, *Zone Therapy* (Century) and on BBC video.

12 Michael York, *Sunday Express* colour supplement, 29th July 1990: p 34.

Chapter 9

1   Sir George Trevelyan, talking to Alternatives (the New Age group which meets at St James' Church, Piccadilly) on 30th July 1990, on 'The Transforming Power of Poetry'.

Chapter 10

1 There was a short ritual on Friday, 15th September 1989, involving a pilgrimage of many faiths which included biblical material from Psalms and Proverbs but no mention of Jesus.

2 William Bloom's books: *Sacred Times; Devas, Fairies and Angels, a Modern Approach; Leylines and Ecology* (with Marko Pogacnik); *Meditation in a Changing World* (all Findhorn Press).

3 Bhagavad Gita has no official part in the Vedas, the sacred canon of Hinduism, but it is the widest read and best loved of Hindu scriptures.

Chapter 12

1 *Martial Arts* leaflet (plus many other similar leaflets), Christian Response to the Occult, PO Box 150, Bromley, Kent.

2 The Bach largo was actually played to Count Kayserling by harpsichord player Johann Goldberg, and it became known as the *Goldberg Variations*.

3 Eileen Campbell and J.H. Brennan in *The Aquarian Guide to the New Age* (The Aquarian Press, Thorsons Publishing, Northamptonshire, 1990), p 43, state that Dr Georgi Lozanov of Bulgaria conducted a 'laboratory study of the *Goldberg Variations* and discovered that the area with which they began and ended had the effect of slowing down certain body processes'.

4 Clive Manning, 'Music of a New Age', *Church of England Newspaper* (15th June 1990), p 12.

Chapter 13

1 Eileen Caddy, *Flight to Freedom* (Element Books: Dorset, in association with Findhorn Press, 1988), p 9.

2 *ibid* p 191: 'I had never taught the boys to say prayers, and we had never read the Bible together. We never imposed our spiritual life on the boys and I hadn't even taught them to meditate, to go within and listen for God's voice.' To put this in context, Eileen explains this when writing to apologise to her son for not being a better mother. The

son responds by telling her not to be so silly and that she was the best mother a boy could have.

3   *ibid* p 25.
4   *ibid* pp 28–29.
5   *ibid* p 31.
6   *ibid* p 32.
7   *ibid* p 35.
8   *ibid* pp 41, 66.
9   *ibid* p 62.
10 *ibid* p 99.
11 *ibid* p 89.
12 *ibid* p 90.
13 *ibid* p 93.
14 *ibid* pp 222–3.
15 *ibid* p 225.
16 *ibid* p 187.
17 *ibid* pp 211–12.
18 *ibid* p 211.
19 *ibid* p 227.

Chapter 16
1   This was the famous description of man given by French philosopher and writer Jean-Paul Sartre.
2   Kevin Logan, *Paganism and the Occult* (Kingsway: Eastbourne, 1988).
3   Christian Ecology Party, Secretary, 58 Quest Hills Road, Malvern, Worcs. (£5 subscription).
4   David Icke, *It Doesn't Have to Be Like This* (Green Print, Merlin Press: London, 1990), p 204. Mr Icke resigned as spokesman of the Green Party on 20th March 1991. He had been receiving healing and spirit messages through British medium Betty Shine. He announced that the Greek philosopher Socrates had given him a series of important, world-saving messages, and that in another mediumistic session he was informed that he was the spirit of the Son of God. Mr Icke said he had been given a sort of blueprint for the survival of the world. He had called it The Truth Vibrations, and this would be published soon (May 1991). A new Jesus Christ would be born at the turn of the millennium and be preaching by the year 2020.
5   David Attenborough, *The Living Planet*, final episode.

Appendix

1   Buckingham Palace Press Office confirmed for me newspaper reports that Princess Diana was regularly involved in complementary medicine. The Press Officer preferred this description to 'alternative' and insisted that both the Prince and Princess of Wales had a firm belief in orthodox medicine, though they did complement this with acupuncture. At the time of contacting Buckingham Palace the media were full of stories about Prince Charles taking the healing waters of Glastonbury after a fall from his polo pony. Dickie Arbiter, Assistant Press Secretary to the Queen, wrote to me the following: 'The Princess of Wales does have occasional acupuncture but has never had shaiatsu treatment. In answer to your second question, the Prince of Wales did visit Glastonbury but not to take the waters.'

    Mr Arbiter explained in a subsequent telephone call that the Prince did sip the waters but only in the way that any normal tourist might.

2   The BMA working party investigating alternative therapies began their work in June 1990. Inquiries of this type usually take between eight months and three years to complete.

3   The information in this paragraph came from the edition of BBC Radio 4's *You and Yours* programme broadcast on 1st August 1990.

4   Dr Douglas Calcott LRCP, MRCS, MB, BS is a medical practitioner and was a member of the Faculty of Homeopathy before renouncing the practice as occult. His statement is made in a foreword to Roy Livesey's book, *Understanding Alternative Medicine*.

5   Roy Livesey, *Understanding Alternative Medicine* (Life Changing Books and New Wine Press: Chichester, 1985).

6   Paul C. Reisser MD, Teri K. Reisser and John Weldon, *New Age Medicine* — A Christian perspective on holistic health (IVP: USA, 1987), back cover.

7   Acupuncturists I have questioned accept that acupuncture works extremely well with five to ten per cent of patients, but even then supplementary anaesthetics are needed for major surgery. Paul and Teri Reisser and John Weldon in *New Age Medicine* comment, 'Nearly every patient

receives, in addition to needling, a narcotic or barbiturate injection prior to surgery or a slow drip of narcotic (usually Demerol) into a vein during the operation' (p 67).

8   Some extreme schools detail up to 800 needling points but the vast majority usually work with the lower number of 365.

9   Acupuncturists have lost count of the number of gate theories there have been since R. Melzack and P. Wall introduced the idea in 1965. Professor Wall changed his mind some years afterwards saying, 'My own belief is that…acupuncture anaesthesia is an effective use of hypnosis': *New Scientist*, vol 55 (20th July) 1974: p 130.

10 A.D. Bambridge RGN, BSc, *Acupuncture Investigated* (Diasozo Trust: Kent, 1989).

11 Mike Scott and I were chatting about the occult just before an audience-participation programme was networked from Central TV Studios. He was concerned that we should get over the dangers of the occult, especially after his experience with the psychic surgery programme which he did for Granada Television in the sixties.